making a marriage

making a marriage

7 essentials
for a strong
relationship

compiled & edited by
LARRY R. MORRIS

BEACON HILL PRESS
OF KANSAS CITY

Copyright 2007
by Beacon Hill Press of Kansas City

ISBN-13: 978-0-8341-2301-4
ISBN-10: 0-8341-2301-0

Continuing Lay Training Unit 423.10A

Printed in the
United States of America

Cover Design: Darlene Filley
Interior Design: Sharon Page

Library of Congress Cataloging-in-Publication Data

Making a marriage : 7 essentials for a strong relationship / compiled and edited by Larry R. Morris.
   p. cm.
Includes bibliographical references.
ISBN-13: 978-0-8341-2301-4 (pbk.)
ISBN-10: 0-8341-2301-0 (pbk.)
 1. Marriage—Religious aspects—Christianity. I. Morris, Larry R., 1955-

BV835.M22455 2007
248.8'44—dc22

2006032837

10 9 8 7 6 5 4 3 2 1

Contents

Preface

"It's just not working! Here we are married for less than a year. Our lives are full, but our marriage is empty." What a starting point for a young Christian couple who shares a love for God but find little time to grow the love God has given them for each other.

"The children are gone and so am I" were her last words. Her husband's jaw dropped as she stomped past him and out the door. They had shared 29 years of married life, serving in the community, being present in church, and giving their lives to their children's futures. Now, as soon as the youngest child had graduated from college, the marriage was over.

* * *

With stories like these becoming increasingly common for professing Christians, it is easy to see why many believe that the Christian life makes little or no difference in marital satisfaction and longevity and that the rate of divorce is the same for Christians as non-Christians.

These types of stories are repeated by the many couples who march from marriage to divorce each year. However, in-depth and credible studies reveal that the marriages of Christians whose marriages are founded upon biblical principles and supported by the community of faith are substantially healthier and more satisfying than those of couples who try to make it on their own.

Making a Marriage was written to couples who want to maximize their marital satisfaction. It acknowledges the need for both a vital personal relationship with God and a growing relationship with a local church. *Making a Marriage* addresses the issues faced by new and mature couples from a biblical point of view. Written by educators and licensed practitioners, it is designed to educate, encourage, and promote good marital practices.

Introduction

According to Genesis, God is the author of marriage. Today, given the value that marriage has for children and society, and the increasing rate of divorce among Christians, it is vital that couples intentionally prepare for the lifelong task of building a Christian marriage.

Making a Marriage contains the foundational principles that help build a strong and lasting relationship. It is an excellent resource to help all couples understand the biblical bedrock of marriage so that they can honor their lifelong vows, improve their relationships with their spouses, and counter our culture's destructive influences.

Family Life Ministries, Beacon Hill Press, and Continuing Lay Training have partnered to offer a book that speaks to couples at all stages of the marital journey. Couples will find help whether they are contemplating marriage; struggling with communication, stress, intimacy issues; or just desiring to make a good marriage better.

Making a Marriage is written by educators and recognized experts in the field of marriage and family. You will find that each chapter is well written and characterized by scholarly integrity, scriptural accuracy, and a holiness perspective.

Available as a free download to book purchasers are two leader's guides (one for laity and one for clergy). Each guide is designed to help couples develop healthy marital skills. *Making a Marriage* can be used by couples alone or in small groups. Each guide explores the chapter's subject through illustrations, dialog, and practical exercises.

In addition to the free leader's guides, you will find other helpful resources and tools at www.clt.nazarene.org. One visit and you will see how you, your small group, or your church can be a part of replacing the destructive cultural trends of our society with God's original, committed, eternal bond: marriage.

1 A Biblical Perspective of Marriage

ROGER L. HAHN

SHE WAS THE "BABY GIRL" *raised in a loving, nurturing family. He was the fifth of nine children raised in a stern, unchristian home. She was from the city. He was from the country. She was pampered and cherished. He labored in the fields and struggled for everything he had. She was well educated. He had little opportunity for education beyond high school. She loved classical music. He loved country western.*

They met and got married. She was 19. He was 25. She expected roses and romance. He expected home-cooked meals and compliance.

Statistics would say there is not much hope for this marriage. But both loved God and looked to the Bible for guidance.

The Bible does not have a special section entitled "Biblical Principles for Marriage," so discovering the biblical principles for marriage is not as easy as sitting down and reading the Bible through. In fact, we discover the biblical teachings on marriage as we read through its pages, often hearing the teaching as the background music when the author is talking about other issues. As we read together, let's listen to the more prominent chords in this important background music.

THE OLD TESTAMENT TEACHING ON MARRIAGE

The Old Testament reveals a significant part of its vision of marriage in the opening chapters of Genesis. Some have stated that, more than any other human institution, marriage goes back to the very activity of God in Creation. But before we proceed, let's look at a general outline of how we will approach Genesis.

Genesis 1: The Relationship of Male and Female

Genesis 2: The Question of Marriage

Genesis 3: Sin and Marriage

Genesis 1

Genesis 1 describes human creation as an extension of the very nature of God. The narrator of the first chapter of the Bible tells us that God said, "Let us make humankind in our image, according to our likeness" (Gen. 1:26).[1] The word "humankind" often translated "man" is *adam* in Hebrew. The Hebrew word *adam* means either a human being or humankind. *Adam* is not used to differentiate male from female, though it is often used in Hebrew culture to refer to a male.

The first statement about humankind found in Scripture is that we are created in the image of God. While there is speculation about what "created in the image of God" means, it is at the least a clear affirmation of human worth. That worth applies to any human being, male or female.

In Gen. 1:26 God proposes the creation of humankind. In verse 27 we read, "And God created the human being in his image, in the image of God he created him, male and female he created them." While not yet describing the marriage relationship, this verse clearly differentiates between the genders, male and female, and reveals that they are bound together in a special way. This biblical proclamation underscores that male and female are both fully and equally human. It also states that both male and female participate equally in the image of God. One is not created more in God's image than the other. This is not a bad truth to remember when we are arguing with our spouses about the common gender traits that frustrate us.

Let's explore this important lesson a bit further by looking at a few important verses of Scripture. Verses 28-29 preserve and develop that unity and uniqueness of the male and female through the use of plural pronouns. Verse 28 begins with the comment "God blessed *them* and said to *them*." Notice that it is male and female, together, who receive God's blessing and command.

Next we read the command, "Be fruitful and become numerous and fill up the earth and control it. Manage the fish of the sea and the birds of the air." Notice that this command is also directed to both male and female. Both male and female are commanded to be partners in fulfilling God's command. Clearly, God is speaking of marriage when He commands the male and female to become fruitful and numerous and fill up the earth. This command to produce offspring includes the command to become good stewards of creation. God's earth and resources are to be cared for with the knowledge that they are His, on loan to the couple. Once again, these commands are given to the male and female equally and together. This command is to each of them personally and to them as a united couple. No one can avoid responsibility for stewardship. Each must fulfill his or her stewardship personally.

According to Gen. 1, both husband and wife together are to be obedient to God. It also envisions a sexual relationship that has children as its outcome. However, children are not the ultimate goal of the marriage. According to the scripture, children are a means by which the male and female extend their stewardship of Creation to all that God has made.

Interesting enough, there is no hint of a hierarchy between the male and female in Gen. 1. Together, male and female are to exercise control or dominion (or even lordship) over the created order.

Genesis 2

The creation account of Gen. 2 provides a more specific picture of God's vision for marriage. The plot of chapter 2 moves toward the creation of woman and the vision of a "one flesh" relationship that will become the New Testament model of marriage. Most traditional English translations obscure the development of this plot by confusion between the word "man" meaning *human* and the word "male." You will see what I mean as we look at this passage more closely as it is translated from the Hebrew text. Note especially the italicized words.

Gen. 2:5 states that "there was no human being [*adam*] to work the ground. Then verse 7 declares that "The LORD God fashioned the human [*adam*] of dust from the ground and breathed the breath of life into the nostrils of the human [*adam*], and the human became a living being."

After describing the Garden that God had created, Gen. 2:15 states that the Lord God put the human (*adam*) in the Garden of Eden to do the work of caring for it. Verse 16 notes that the Lord God commanded the human (*adam*) to not eat from the tree of the knowledge of good and evil. A key step in the plot comes in Gen. 2:18 when the Lord God said, "It is not good for the human (*adam*) to be alone. I will make a helper corresponding to the human (*adam*)."

To this point there has been no mention of male or female. It is the human being who is created from the ground and given the task of caring for the ground. It is the human being who should not be alone and for whom God will make a corresponding helper. It is not the male who is alone and needs a helper or the female who is alone and needs a helper. It is the human person—any human person—who is alone and needs a helper. And God promises to make such a helper for the lonely and needy human being.

The promised "helper" is described by the Hebrew word 'ezer. This helper is no secondary or inferior being to come alongside the male to provide support. This is made clear when we look at other passages that use this same word. For example, the Psalms repeatedly name God himself as the helper ('ezer) of

His people. The *'ezer* is a powerful and strong helper who supports and supplies what the other needs.

The fact that the Lord God commits himself to making this helper shows that God recognizes that He himself is not the needed helper. The helper God will provide will be one "corresponding to" the human. One could also translate the phrase "corresponding to" as "parallel to." God will provide a helper parallel to, or on the same level as, the lonely and needy human being. As of yet, neither the word "male" nor "female" has appeared in Gen. 2, and there is no hierarchy of gender mentioned.

In Gen. 2:19-24 we read about the search for this helper. The human (*adam*) is not God's only creation from the ground (*adamah*); all the animals of the field and the birds of the air are also formed from the ground. So the Lord God brings all the animals to the human (*adam*) for the human to name them. Three times Gen. 2:19-20 speaks of the human naming the animals. In the culture of the ancient Semites, naming was an act of domination or subjugating. The narrator concludes in verse 20 that "no helper corresponding to the human was found for the human." Not only are the animals not suitable as a corresponding helper to the human, but also they are clearly inferior to the human who has named them.

This story is nearing its climax. According to verse 21, the Lord God placed the human (*adam*) in a divinely induced sleep and took from the side (or rib) of the human and closed up the flesh. God then built from the side (or rib) of the human a woman (*isha*) and brought her to the man (*adam*), according to verse 22. It is not until this point of the plot that the different genders are mentioned. Let's look at the some of the dialog.

The man (*adam*) responds in verse 23 to the woman with recognition and affirmation that they belong to each other: "At last! This is bone of my bone, flesh of my flesh. She will be called woman [*isha*] because she was taken from man [*ish*]!" Verse 23 is a loud affirmation that God's helper is custom-made for fellowship with the man.

The scripture then concludes in Gen. 2:24 with the statement that the man (*ish*) will leave father and mother and unite himself with his woman (*isha*) and that they will become one flesh. The obvious conclusion is that marriage is the purpose of God's creation of male and female. The Hebrew word usually translated "join" or "unite" or "cling to" in verse 24 is used in the Old Testament of tying objects together, of buckling a belt, of close associations, and of continuing relationships. It implies both the closeness and the permanence of the relationship.

Verse 24 also states some of the most memorable words describing the biblical view of marriage: "They will become one flesh." Part of the meaning of becoming one flesh refers to sexual union and the children who are the result. But no Hebrew person of the biblical period would have limited the one-flesh vision to simply physical or sexual union. Flesh represented the whole person with physical, spiritual, emotional, and intellectual dimensions.

To become one flesh, in a biblical way, speaks of a couple coming together in all the dimensions of life to complement each other so that together they are a stronger whole than either of them is individually. To become one flesh does not mean that each partner contributes equally in every dimension of life.

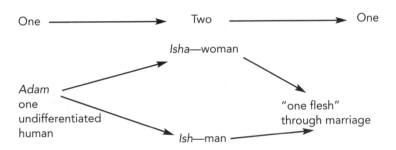

Rather, each partner gives himself or herself completely to the marriage and has made the marriage more important than any other human relationship (such as that of father and mother).

Becoming one flesh brings back together the man (*ish*) and the woman (*isha*) who was differentiated by God in the creation of the woman. Thus Gen. 1—2 paints a picture of human creation that simply begins with the human being (*adam*) whom God differentiates into woman (*isha*) and man (*ish*) and then reunites into one flesh, the marriage couple. Without devaluing or dehumanizing persons who are single either by or against their own choice, Genesis portrays what it means to be human as a movement from one to two to one.

To be fully human in the Hebrew mind is to be both sexually differentiated as a male or female and to be united via marriage. This unity of male and female in marriage contains all God designed humanity to be. The statement of Gen. 2:18 stands, "It is not good for a human to be alone." Marriage provides the most common and hoped for means by which God's vision of persons becoming fully human can be fulfilled.[2]

The final statement of Gen. 2 is also important for understanding God's vision for marriage. Verse 25 concludes the chapter with the comment "The two of them were naked, the human [*adam*] and his woman [*isha*], and they experienced no shame." Given the normal Old Testament concerns for nudity and shame, this is a dramatic statement of vulnerability and trust. This verse envisions a marriage characterized by complete openness and trust. Such a relationship can never be one-sided. It is the picture of both partners placing themselves—emotionally, spiritually, physically, and intellectually—in the hands of the other in the confidence that they will not be betrayed or hurt.

Genesis 3

Gen. 3 reveals that the fall turned God's vision of marriage upside down. The immediate result of the first couple's disobedience of God's one command is awareness of their nakedness and shame (vv. 7, 10). Disobedience destroyed the mutual vulnerability and trust that had been the climax of God's creation of marriage. The sense of mutuality and partnership that was so central to God's vision for marriage is lost. The consequence of disobedience specifically for the woman would be pain in childbearing (v. 16). Thus the most intimate expression of one flesh—sexual union—would lead to pain because of sin.

Further, the woman's man (*ish*) would rule or have dominion over her. Another result of sin is the loss of mutuality and a complementary relationship. In its place come domination, hierarchy, and the struggle for power. The scripture illustrates this truth in Gen. 3:20, though one must understand the culture to recognize the significance of his comment. "The man [*adam*] called the name of his woman [*isha*] Eve." In ancient Semitic culture, naming another was an act of domination or power, claiming the authority to define and determine the fate of the one named. Remember that the man had not named the woman prior to the fall. Naming her was the first act of subjugating her.

Gen. 3 also marks the transition from God's vision of marriage to descriptions of marriages in the Old Testament. It is at this point that we must consider what will determine our vision of marriage. Will we choose to make the results of the fall—marriages characterized by hierarchy, conflict, power struggles, lack of vulnerability and intimacy, and domination—the goal toward which we strive in our marriages? Or will we choose the vision of marriage characterized by love, companionship, trust, intimacy, mutuality, for which God created human beings as our vision and goal? Surely people who believe that God's sanctifying power can renew the divine image within us cannot be satisfied with a vision of marriage determined by sin and the fall.

As people who believe in God's transforming and sanctifying power, we must live above the sociological, psychological, and cultural expectations of marriage. Regardless of what our culture teaches us about marriage, holy people stand under the call of God. We are to live out our marriages in mutuality, complementing each other's strengths and weaknesses, being both vulnerable and trusting, discovering safety, and reverently receiving the gifts of intimacy.

Marriage Covenant

One should not suppose that a vision of marriage disappears from the Old Testament with Gen. 3. There are examples of marriages in which we can catch a glimpse of couples aspiring toward God's vision of marriage. There are moments in which the marriages of Abraham and Sarah, Isaac and Rebecca, Jacob and Rachel, and Ruth and Boaz reflect God's vision of marriage. But unfortunately more often than not we discover the pull of sin and a fallen culture turning marriages into mere contracts and destructive struggles for power. That is no doubt why early in the Hebrew culture it became necessary to develop laws for divorce to keep married people from completely destroying each other.

Though hints are present in Gen. 2, it is not until we arrive at the final book of the Old Testament that we find marriage described as a covenant. The Hebrew text of Malachi 2:14, 16, is difficult to understand, but the underlying assumption of marriage as a covenant is clear.

So what is a covenant? The biblical concept of covenant is a way of describing a relationship. The covenant most often mentioned in the Old Testament is the Sinai covenant between God and Israel. This covenant described the relationship of God and Israel in terms of their shared story (or history), their shared expectations, and the consequences that would come if the expectations were not met. These characteristics of the Sinai covenant also apply to a marriage covenant.

Shared Story

The covenant established between God and Israel on Mt. Sinai began by the reviewing of their shared story (summarized in Exod. 20:2) and by God's declaration that He is the one who brought Israel out of Egypt. Just as the historical events that brought God and Israel together to establish a covenant, a marriage covenant is built on the memories of shared stories. Many modern counselors advise persons to strengthen their marriages by reviewing and reenacting the events that brought the couple together.

Mutual Expectations

The Ten Commandments, as well as the many statutes and ordinances found in Exod. 20—23, constitute the expectations that defined the covenant relationship between God and Israel. The Old Testament often summarized those expectations with the words of God "I will be your God, and you will be my people." This statement reveals the mutuality of the covenant agreement. Israel, as God's people, was to fulfill a set of expectations. And God, as Israel's divine ruler, was to fulfill a set of expectations to Israel. In similar fashion, the marriage covenant is built around mutual expectations. When the expectations become one-sided, the covenant is threatened.

Consequences

The covenant between God and Israel included a section sometimes described as "blessings and curses" (example: Deut. 27—28) and points out the consequences of keeping or breaking covenant. Just as the Sinai covenant had consequences, so does the marriage covenant. In fact, the point of Mal. 2:10-16 is that breaking faith in one's marriage covenant has the consequence of undermining Israel's worship. Failure to maintain mutuality and vulnerability in marriage has negative spiritual consequences in terms of one's ability to relate intimately to God.

Whether you get your vision of marriage by looking at creation or the covenant contract, the Old Testament presents a high view of marriage. And fidelity, mutuality, intimacy, trust, and vulnerability are the key elements in this vision of marriage. One could easily conclude this biblical vision of marriage is too high, that it is impossible for normal human beings living in a sinful world to be in such a relationship. However, before we jump to such a conclusion, first acknowledge that this view of marriage is based upon couples who are obedient to God and who exercise a great deal of grace toward each other. These two factors are essential and crucial.

THE NEW TESTAMENT PERSPECTIVE ON MARRIAGE

The New Testament teachings on marriage are grounded firmly in the Old Testament. Four times Gen. 2:24 is quoted in the New Testament—twice by Jesus in the Gospels and twice by Paul in his letters. Other than 1 Pet. 3:1-7, all the explicit teachings on marriage in the New Testament are in the gospel passages by Jesus and letter passages from Paul. Jesus' teachings on marriage come in the context of discussions of divorce thrust upon Him by adversaries or enemies.

Divorce was a hot topic during Jesus' time. As a result, people asked about His position on divorce on a number of occasions. Jesus' answers to these questions appear in the Gospels of Matthew and Mark. Unfortunately, no one asked Jesus about what constituted a good marriage.

Matt. 19:3-12 and Mark 10:2-12 appear to be describing the same event, though the two gospels do not record the conversation in exactly the same way. Both gospels begin with a question from the Pharisees designed to "test" Jesus. The question was "Is it lawful for a man to divorce his wife?" Matt. 19:3 adds the words "for any and every reason." The context of the question was the ongoing debate between two rival schools of the Pharisees on the subject of divorce. Both groups appealed to Deut. 24:1-4, which speaks of a husband giving his wife a certificate of divorce when she finds no favor (or grace) in his eyes because there is some "indecent matter" regarding her. The two groups or schools, Hillel and Shammai, debated what that "indecent matter" might be.

The school of Shammai considered the indecent matter to be sexual or marital infidelity. The school of Hillel took a much broader view of the issue and interpreted it to be as simple as poor cooking, housekeeping, or the lack of attractiveness. Clearly the school of Hillel had a very low view of marriage, trivializing it to the point that a man who saw a more attractive woman than his wife was permitted to divorce his wife to marry the other, more attractive, woman.

When Jesus was asked about the reasons a man could divorce his wife, He turned the focus from Deut. 24 back to Gen. 1—2. His response is recorded in Matt. 19:4, where He recites Gen. 1:27—God created male and female. He then quotes Gen. 2:24, which calls on a man to leave father and mother, be joined to his wife, and that the two will become one flesh. Jesus then comments, "As a result they are no longer two, but one flesh. Therefore, what God has yoked together mankind must not separate" (Matt. 19:6).

Jesus reaffirms the vision for marriage first given in Genesis and describes marriage as the yoking together of the husband and wife by God. The image of God yoking the husband and wife together is instructive. First, this illustration eliminates any sense of hierarchy in the marriage. Two oxen are yoked side by side. They work parallel to each other and in step with each other. Second, there is a hierarchy and subjugation (to God). The married couple is to be subject to God as the one who places the yoke of marriage upon them. Lest we think this imagery portrays marriage as a terrible burden (yoke), the Jews of Jesus' time spoke of the covenant as a yoke. And Jesus described discipleship as taking his yoke (Matt. 11:28-30). Therefore, Jesus views marriage as a mutual and complementary relationship in which both partners are subject to God.

Jesus also states that persons must not separate what God has joined together. The Greek grammar is stronger than most English translations of Matt. 19:6 imply. We could say that Jesus declared that it was imperative that people not separate what God has yoked together. In simple and direct terms, Jesus was teaching the indissolubility of marriage.

Jesus' teaching is appealing to happily married people. Persons who are unhappily married or who have a low view of marriage find the idea of an indissoluble marriage harsh and restrictive. The Pharisees speak from such a perspective with their question in Matt. 19:7. Jesus' reply is important. He states that Moses permitted divorce because of the hardness of human hearts but that divorce was never God's intention for marriage.

It is important to recognize what Jesus is doing in this passage. He does not prohibit divorce; rather, He names it for what it is—a failure to achieve God's intention for marriage because of human sinfulness and brokenness. In this way Jesus affirms an extremely high view of marriage but acknowledges that human beings may sometimes find themselves in circumstances where that high view of marriage cannot be realized because of sin and brokenness.

This teaching corresponds with people's experience. No emotionally healthy person celebrates divorce, but sometimes such a person recognizes that because of sin and human brokenness divorce is the less evil of two choices—neither of which was God's or the person's original intention.[3]

The Apostle Paul's Teachings on Marriage

Paul's teaching on marriage appears in most concentrated form in 1 Cor. 7 and Eph. 5:22-31. Both passages are complex and have generated as much confusion as help. They are part of the reason many people question Paul's view of marriage.

First Cor. 7:1 contains the provocative statement "It is good for a man to not touch a woman." This would certainly suggest a low view of marriage on Paul's part. However, verse 1 begins with the words "Now concerning the things about which you wrote." These words begin a section extending at least through 1 Cor. 14, in which the apostle responds to issues raised by the Corinthians in a letter sent to him. It is most likely that the words "It is good for a man to not touch a woman" are a quotation from the Corinthian letter, because Paul's words in the following verses portray a different view of marriage.

The apostle's response in verse 2 is that each man should have his own wife and each woman should have her own husband. The reason for this is for the prevention of sexual immorality.[4] Verse 3 declares that each husband must meet his obligation to his wife and that each wife must meet her obligation to her husband. The reason for this is stated in verse 4: "The wife does not have authority over her own body, but her husband does. Likewise the husband does not have authority over his own body, but his wife does."

The immediate context suggests that the obligation spouses owe each other is a sexual relationship. However, the larger context suggests that the obligation includes all that comes under the vision of marriage presented in Gen. 2. A husband owes his wife all his physical, sexual, emotional, spiritual, and intellectual abilities, and the wife owes her husband all her physical, sexual, emotional, spiritual, and intellectual abilities. Especially surprising in verses 3-4 is the complete mutuality of this obligation between husbands and wives. Given the customs of Jewish culture and the practices of Greek and Roman society, Paul's words requiring complete mutuality are astounding.

The apostle appears to be addressing individuals at Corinth who regarded sexual activity, even within marriage, as degrading or unspiritual. Paul was concerned that married persons who take such an approach would place inappropriate sexual pressure on their spouses. Therefore, he forbids married believers to deprive their spouses of sexual relations even for the purpose of prayer (verse 5) except for short periods of time and by mutual consent.

Several times in chapter 7 Paul recommends singleness and celibacy for those who are able (gifted). The purpose of such a decision is to increase one's dedication to ministry. First Cor. 7:29-35 states that married persons have obligations to their spouses and families. Single persons are free to devote themselves to evangelism without distraction. Paul believed singleness was a good choice in light of his confidence that "the time has become shortened."

Paul believed the Second Coming was imminent, so he believed that singleness was a more efficient way to prepare for Christ's return than marriage. We can grant the correctness of Paul's logic while admitting that his assumption about the timing of the Second Coming was clearly wrong.

In 1 Cor. 7:10-11 Paul forbids divorce between believing spouses. He also counters the arguments of Corinthians who recommended that Christians divorce unbelieving spouses. Paul states in verses 12-13 that the believing spouse must remain with an unbelieving spouse as long as the unbelieving spouse is willing to remain in the relationship.

Verse 14 provides an amazing argument. The unbelieving spouse is sanctified by the believing spouse. Paul believed that by living together in marriage, holiness could flow from a believer to an unbeliever! He viewed the believing spouse as God's agent, embodying holiness, incarnating Christ, and helping to bring salvation to the unbeliever. Many of us have witnessed how the contagious and attractive life of a believing spouse has been effective in bringing the unbelieving mate to Christ.[5]

Taking a Closer Look at Paul's Teaching on Marriage

The highest view of marriage from Paul appears in Eph. 5:22-33. This scripture has often been used to demonstrate that wives should be subject to husbands. However, careful reading of the Greek text raises significant questions about this view. Let's see if we can walk through this together.

Modern English translations are consistent in placing an imperative such as "submit" or "be subject" or "submit yourselves" or "be subordinate" or "yield" in verse 22, directing wives to submit to their husbands. However, it comes as quite a surprise to discover that there is no such verb in the Greek text. That's right—there is no verb at all in the Greek text! The reason translators supply a verb such as "submit" in verse 22 is that the preceding verse uses it.

Verse 21 speaks of "submitting to one another in the fear of Christ." However, the submission described there is a mutual submission and not the submission of one gender to another. Paul's treatment of marriage immediately follows his teaching about mutual submission and the Spirit-filled life. This implies that Paul views marriage as an arena in which mutual submission is lived out.[6]

Paul's statement in verse 23 that the husband is head of the wife as Christ is head of the Church surely does not imply that the husband is authorized to dominate his wife.[7] Christ does not behave that way toward the Church; He loves and serves the Church. That love was characterized by Christ giving himself for the Church, sanctifying it, purifying it, dying for it. Christ's goal was to present the Church as glorious, without spot or wrinkle or any defect, but as holy and blameless.

Verse 28 brings us back to the subject at hand: "Thus, in this way husbands ought to love their own wives as they love their own bodies." First, this passage calls on husbands to love their wives as Christ loved the Church. Second, this verse points us back to Gen. 2 and the story of the creation of woman. To love one's wife is to love one's own body, because woman was created out of the side (or rib) of man and in marriage the two become one flesh.

The example of Christ and the Church and the relationship of husbands and wives are intertwined in verse 29. Paul writes, "No man ever hated his own flesh but nourishes and cherishes it." At one level this simply means that no normal man hates himself or destroys his own body. Rather, he takes care of himself and has healthy self-respect and even pride. At a second level of meaning, if the husband and wife become one flesh in marriage as Gen. 2:24 states, then a man cannot be hateful or destructive toward his wife, because she is his own flesh. He must nourish and cherish her as he would himself, because they are one flesh.

Some people have noticed that in this passage of Scripture Paul so intertwines the subject of Christ and the Church and the relationship of husbands and wives that we might wonder if he has lost track of the main subject. And that may be the significant point he is making—that the best example of how Christ relates to the church is found in a godly marriage.

So how do we understand and apply this passage in our culture, a culture vastly different from that to which Paul originally wrote? The cultural expectation of the first century was that wives would submit to their husbands and that husbands would use their wives for their own sexual and social gratification. In that context Paul could assume that wives were submissive and that the husbands were the ones in need of major instruction. However, the point of the whole paragraph is to show how marriage can be an example, an expression of the mutual submission demonstrated by the presence of the Holy Spirit in the Church.

Surely the application is not that one gender is to submit and one gender is to love. Rather, the application is that our marriages are to be an example of the relationship that exists between Christ and the Church. Both parties are to love and submit. To those who argue that "somebody has to be in charge of the home" Paul might well respond, "Yes, Christ must be in charge of the home." And if Christ is Lord of the home, then mutual submission and mutual love are possible and ultimately inevitable.

Conclusion

We sometimes forget that the Bible was written in a particular culture and time in history quite different from our own. The culturally embedded nature of the Bible means that its principles and visions are cast in terms best understood in that time and place. To move from quoting the Bible to appropriately applying it to contemporary culture will always be a challenge.

Actually, when we consider the world in which the Bible was written, the character of its vision of marriage is amazing. How could such a lofty vision of marriage come from a time in which marriages were so harsh? Surely, the picture of marriage found in the Bible is testimony to the Scriptures' inspiration by the Holy Spirit.

Ultimately, at the heart of the biblical view of marriage is Gen. 2:24. Its message is timeless: a person must leave father and mother and be joined together with his or her spouse so that they become one flesh. This union is to result in each spouse nourishing and cherishing the other with the holiness and well-being of the other being a first concern.

Surely a marriage built on this biblical view would be delightful and fulfilling. The real question is whether it is possible. And the answer to that question depends on one's confidence in the grace of God to transform human lives. John Wesley often claimed that God does not command what His grace does not enable. God's grace is sufficient even to enable the kind of marriage envisioned in Scripture.

Remember our beginning illustration?

She was the "baby girl" raised in a loving, nurturing Christian family. He was the fifth of nine children raised in a stern, unchristian home until he was 12. She was from the city. He was from the country. She was pampered and cherished. He labored in the fields and struggled for everything he had. She was well educated. He had little opportunity for education beyond high school. She loved classical music. He loved country western.

They met at church. She was a Christian. He was a Christian. She fell in love with this handsome, young man with the Southern drawl. He fell in love with this cute little naïve girl he called, "Angel Girl." They got married. She was 19. He was 25. She expected roses and romance. He expected home-cooked meals and compliance.

Statistics would say there is not much hope for this marriage.

This couple would say, "If not for our vow to follow Christ and our commitment to place Jesus as Lord of our relationship, the statistics would be right." This Christian couple celebrated their 40th anniversary in 2006.

God makes all things possible!

Endnotes

1. All translation of individual Scripture passages is by the author.

2. Single persons, regardless of the cause of their singleness, also need a means by which to become significantly, nonsexually, connected to another person.

3. The account found in Mark 10:2-12 proceeds in the opposite order. The subject of Moses' allowance of divorce and Deut. 24 come up first, and afterward Jesus proceeds to teach God's original intention for marriage from Gen. 1 and 2. The two gospels give the same content but in a different order. The order in Mark makes it clear that Jesus gives priority to the teaching of Genesis over that of Deuteronomy. In the biblical world, that which was older was considered to be more valuable or more important. Thus the theological vision of Gen. 1—2 is more important and more binding than the provisions of Deut. 24, which came later to provide a way of dealing with the results of human sinfulness.

4. The word for sexual immorality, *porneia*, is plural. Apparently Paul believed the many instances of sexual immorality suggest that persons should be married.

5. While some of Paul's thoughts on marriage in 1 Cor. 7 seem utilitarian or simply pragmatic, here we see that he believed that marriage can be evangelistic.

6. The first example Paul uses to illustrate the meaning of submission is that of a wife to her husband, introduced in verse 22. Though there is no verb in the Greek text, the verb "submit" is clearly implied. What is not implied is that it should be understood as an imperative or a command. Rather, the flow of thought suggests that it should be understood as a simple indicative, a statement of fact. This submission was culturally assumed in Paul's time. So instead of Paul being interpreted as demanding that wives submit to husbands, the Greek text reads that the submission of wives given to husbands is an example of the way all Christians submit to each other.

7. The concept of "head" in biblical thought more often refers to the source of something rather than to authority over someone. Therefore, verse 23 reminds readers of the creation of woman in Gen. 2, in which the man was the source from which woman was created. Likewise, Christ is the source from which the Church flows. The first imperative in this passage comes in verse 25 with the command for husbands to love their wives as Christ loved the Church. The submission of wives to husbands practiced in the culture of that time provides an example of the mutual submission that shows we are filled with the Holy Spirit. However, the treatment of wives by husbands in that time fell short. So Paul had to command husbands to demonstrate their mutual submission by loving their wives with the kind of love Christ demonstrated for the Church.

Roger L. Hahn is dean and professor of New Testament at Nazarene Theological Seminary, Kansas City. Dr. Hahn has a long and prestigious history as an educator and has served as an educator since 1974. He is also a highly sought-after author and frequently writes theological exposes, commentaries, books, and Sunday School curriculum. He currently serves as teaching pastor of the Word and Table worship service at Kansas City First Church of the Nazarene. He is also a sought-after speaker for revivals and retreats.

Books include *Discovering the New Testament* (Beacon Hill Press of Kansas City), *A Commentary on the Gospel of Matthew* (Wm. B. Eerdmans Publishing Company), *Finding True Fulfillment in the Crush of Life* (Beacon Hill Press of Kansas City), *Great Passages of the Bible: Salvation from Beginning to End* (Beacon Hill Press of Kansas City), *The End: How Are We to Face the End of Time and the Beginning of Eternity?* (Beacon Hill Press of Kansas City),

2 Seven Commitments of a Lasting Marriage

DAVID AND LISA FRISBIE

"WE'RE NOT PLANNING TO GET MARRIED," Corinne explains to a close friend. "We both love each other too much for that! After all, most marriages end in divorce anyway, so why bother with a meaningless ceremony?"

Corinne's friend nods her head in agreement. "My mom just got divorced again—for the third time," she says with a sigh. "I feel really sad for her."

Welcome to relational life in the 21st century. Today many couples choose to cohabit without making a moral, legal, spiritual, or personal commitment. Across western Europe and throughout North America, couples of all ages see marriage as an optional—but perhaps not helpful—approach to living together. In the mindset of many, the Church's insistence on marriage is often viewed as an archaic, legalistic requirement that imposes discipline without providing benefits. Why get married today if the likely result is divorce tomorrow?

Against this backdrop of changing moral values, we have been researching the marital satisfaction of long-term, married couples. We have examined the dynamics of personal and marital fulfillment of marriages. We have explored the nuts and bolts of relationships, searching for the reasons some marriages go the distance while others do not. As we explored these issues, one word surfaced again and again from marriage partners who reported a high level of personal satisfaction and fulfillment in their relationship: "commitment."

From our research it became apparent almost immediately that the meaning of the word "commitment" varied, even between two life partners who reported a positive experience in their marriage. After gathering, processing, and evaluating the comments and stories of these successful couples, we put together seven descriptions they used to illustrate commitment within the context of their relationship. Ranked in no particular order, these seven aspects of commitment were cited as reasons for success by these highly satisfied, deeply fulfilled marriage partners.

1. Commitment to seeing marriage the way God sees it.

Contented couples believe that marriage was God's idea in the first place. Rather than speaking in legalistic terms (God insists we stay married), these couples told us that marriage was part of God's original design for the universe. In other words, when God created man and woman, He created them to dwell together within a marriage relationship, living with each other in an abiding, lifetime commitment.

Couples often referred to Gen. 2:24, in which the writer describes the marriage model of a man leaving his father and mother to become united with his wife. In this, the Bible's earliest telling of the human story, the husband and the wife become one. It's a theme that becomes clear throughout the Old and New Testaments. When questioned about divorce, Jesus reiterated God's original viewpoint: "'Haven't you read,' he replied, 'that at the beginning the Creator "made them male and female," and said "For this reason a man will leave his father and mother and be united to his wife, and the two will become one flesh"? So they are no longer two, but one. Therefore what God has joined together, let man not separate'" (Matt. 19:4-6).

God's design? Contemporary couples need to hear Jesus' words. Many believe that marriage is a social custom imposed by the Church rather than a spiritual heritage we receive by the loving purpose of a creative God. Couples committed to a long-term marriage see it differently. "This is God's best," Walter said, talking about his 42-year marriage to Sylvia. "This is what God had in mind when He created both man and woman. We are made for each other, literally." As Walter talked about his own marriage, he cited Gen. 2. "The two of us have become one in our relationship," he said. "It's not just an idea or a concept; it's a living truth at the center of our married life."

From God's perspective, becoming married creates wholeness and togetherness that is intentional and healthy, fulfilling God's original intention. Husbands and wives are designed for a loving and lasting unity. Deeply fulfilled couples often speak of this reality. They do so with passion and intensity, describing an incarnational truth they have explored together on a journey *through* life that they see as a journey *for* life. God's design, say these couples, is an ongoing marriage union that transcends the separateness of two individual lives and becomes an authentic and unified whole for a man and a woman together. Happy couples find evidence that this design is hard-wired into the universe in addition to its being part of the biblical record.

2. Commitment to marriage as a lifelong connection.

Jared is a naturalist who serves as a forest ranger in rural Montana. "Look at the snow geese," Jared said as we talked with him about his marriage. "They're such beautiful creatures. I've never found one that was reading the Bible, yet somehow they know they should mate for life! If geese can figure it out, why can't the rest of us?"

Jared, married for three years, reports a high degree of fulfillment within his marriage. Amy, six months pregnant, has the same view. "We're in this thing for life," she said. "We weren't in a hurry to get married, because both of us look at it the same way—once you get married, you stay married until death parts you. That's what the traditional vows say about it: 'until death parts us.'"

Jared nodded in agreement. "We've both seen a lot of divorces among our friends and family. I'm not judging any of their lives—it's just that Amy and I have a much different view of marriage. For us, it means we are totally committed to each other for as long as we both shall live."

"This is for life," Grant stated, echoing Jared's view. "It's not about trying each other on for size. This is for better or worse and in sickness or health. Regardless of what happens, Melissa and I will stay together for as long as we're both alive."

This is how satisfied couples tend to look at the marriage relationship. Easier said than done? Perhaps. Yet happily, married couples often report that how they see marriage is a major component of their satisfaction. Thinking of their marriage as permanent tends to create the conditions under which a secure, highly fulfilling relationship can blossom and thrive.

"I grew up thinking that all men leave," Melissa sighed. "I had seen my dad and then a stepdad I really loved leave my mom after only a few years together. I knew that if I ever got married, I wanted more than that—a lot more. I wanted either to stay single or stay married for life. I wanted something my mom never really got—a man who stayed."

Married for 11 years and the parents of three growing children, Grant and Melissa both explained that staying married for life is a key factor in their current happiness. "Whatever we need to work on, we'll work on," Grant affirmed. "We've had some issues already, and we'll probably have more issues later. Life is like that. But we'll work on whatever comes, side by side. We are staying together. We're married for life—no exceptions."

It's a theme we hear often from satisfied couples. When they talk about commitment, these couples mean that they will be together for life, no matter what. They are serious about staying together until death—and only death—parts them.

3. Commitment to the high value of keeping promises.

Cindy had been married for just 18 months when clinical depression struck, changing her personality and even her appearance. Diagnosed as severely afflicted, she spent much of the next three years seeking and receiving treatment, often heavily medicated and once briefly hospitalized. Did her husband, Mark, ever think of leaving her? "Not for a minute," he insists as we interviewed him. "I made a promise. I was raised to believe that a person's word is what shows his or her true character. In my family, we learned at an early age to be careful about making promises. And when you make a promise, you keep a promise."

Mark's family is not unique despite much current evidence to the contrary. As we talked with long-term, happily married couples, we often discovered their life experiences had been stressful, frustrating, and at times disastrous. Yet for these couples, even going through great difficulties, their marital satisfaction remained high.

Can a couple really remain joyously married in spite of severe trauma? Mark didn't hesitate as he emphatically exclaimed, "Absolutely. When you always keep your promises to people, they learn to trust you and have confidence in you. And nothing builds a relationship like trust. That's true in life, and it's true in marriage."

Cindy nodded in agreement as her husband continued. "I promised Cindy I would stay by her side," Mark explained. "She made the same kind of promise to me. If I had been the one who was hurting, or if I was in the hospital, Cindy would have stood by me all the way. In our case, she was the one suffering, and I was the one staying committed to her and helping her get through it. But it would have worked out the same either way. Both of us are committed to keeping our word."

The power of kept promises builds a strong sense of security and permanence in a relationship. As Mark's commitment reminded us, a person's character reveals itself when the challenges and obstacles of life must be faced head-on. Knowing that your partner is a promise-keeper helps you relax into a place of safety, even as the world around you brings unexpected suffering and disappointment. Contented couples are promise-keepers; they speak of promises made and kept when describing what commitment means in their marriages.

4. Commitment to accountability.

When we first met Gary and Jayne, they were living separately. Married for nine years, they had experienced conflict almost from the beginning of their marriage. Now, two children and nearly a decade later, both of them were tired of fighting.

"We just need some time away from each other right now to work on our issues" is how Jayne explained their decision. "My counselor told us that being apart would really help us figure out our relationship. We're doing this to strengthen our marriage, not to end it."

Although Gary quickly tired of living on his own and being able to visit his home and his children only on Jayne's terms, he went along with the plan. He hoped for a positive, long-term outcome despite his short-term daily pain. Six months later, claiming to be reluctant, Jayne filed for divorce. As a general observation, married couples who experiment with living apart tend to drift farther apart rather than drawing closer together during their time of separation.

By contrast, married couples who choose to work on their issues together most often remain together, especially if they involve a network of supporters to whom they are accountable for the choices and decisions they make as they resolve their differences.

Bob and Rosa are an example of a couple headed for a separation who chose to become accountable to trusted family members. In their case, having a support network helped them avoid living separately. It's a decision that may also have helped them avoid a divorce.

"We were fighting all the time," Rosa shared. "We just couldn't quit arguing with each other. Sometimes it was over nothing! Sometimes it was a big issue or an important choice. But all we did was fight." Rosa received counsel from several coworkers who advised her to try living apart for a while and working on the marriage while living separately. Bob was willing to live apart if it would be helpful. Almost as an afterthought, the couple decided to sit down and talk with some trusted family members and seek their opinion on the matter. Bob and Rosa turned to his older sister and her younger sister, both of whom had played prominent roles in their wedding.

Bob's older sister had functioned almost as a second mother for Bob and was quick to negate the living separately idea. "That's how couples end up divorced!" Bob's sister exclaimed. "Don't even think about trying that. You're a married couple, and that means you work on your problems together and you solve them together!"

Rosa's sister gave exactly the same advice. "Don't start living separate lives," she said. "You need to be growing together instead of further apart. Keep on living together and get the help you need. See a Christian counselor. Join a small group. Call your pastor. But whatever you do, do it together and not apart."

Bob and Rosa decided to look around for a small group that might be helpful. They looked no farther than their own church, which had many groups available for couples. "We found one about growing a marriage," Bob says, "so we called the group leader. That telephone call changed our lives." Three weeks after nearly separating, Bob and Rosa attended a Tuesday night meeting a few miles from their home. With four other couples they shared coffee, a brief Bible study, and a lengthy discussion about married life.

"It was exactly what we needed," recounted Rosa. "We found that we weren't alone, that other couples were trying to learn to communicate better and solve their problems without fighting. Until that night we felt like failures in our marriage. Both of us had been thinking we were losing it and that we just couldn't keep it together. Sitting there in a circle around the Harrises' living room, we found that we weren't alone."

Our research consistently shows that when couples connect with family members and friends and build a support network with the goal of saving their relationship, then good things begin to happen. Like Bob and Rosa, such couples soon discover their problems and issues may be typical in a marriage. Good things happen when troubled couples ask other Christian adults to mentor and encourage them in enhancing their marriages.

One couple described this to us as "willingness to be transparent" in their relationship. "We realized that we needed to let other people know how we were doing," Carolyn stated matter-of-factly. "We were having trouble with our communication, and nobody else really knew about it. We could see ourselves drifting apart. We decided to join a Bible study group with the goal of making some close friends. We hoped somebody would have some ideas we could try."

Carolyn and her husband became acquainted with a couple with whom they felt relaxed and comfortable.

"We invited them to dinner first," Carolyn remembers. "Then they invited us to a backyard barbecue at their house. As we got to know them, we could tell they were happy together—something we wanted. We started by watching and listening to them as they talked to each other. I began asking Ellen some questions about her marriage, and she was very open and honest in her answers to me. I began to realize that many couples have problems communicating and that it takes time and work before a couple can really understand each other. When we felt comfortable, we shared what we were going through. They didn't preach, judge, or take sides. Sometimes they would even say 'We don't know what to tell you,' which actually encouraged us. We began to notice our marriage was getting better. Not only were we fighting less, but also we had learned some nicer and kinder ways to work through our disagreements.

"I don't know where we would be today without those two. But I think we were heading for a divorce like so many other people. I think if we had kept our problems to ourselves or had tried to solve our problems by living apart, we would have drifted apart forever."

Being accountable to others, especially to Christian friends and family members who share the value of protecting and preserving a marriage relationship, can help a couple stay committed to each other while working through their issues. Building a support network is an excellent way to reinforce your commitment to stay together and grow a healthy marriage.

The presence of caring friends who serve as ongoing advisors and prayer partners can help a couple weather the storms of life while remaining together.

5. Commitment to blessing children with an intact nuclear family.

When Andy called for a family meeting one Saturday morning, his kids thought Dad was announcing some good news. Facing his wife and three kids in the kitchen, Andy dropped his bombshell with very little fanfare and almost no explanation.

"I need my space for a while," Andy announced at the family meeting. "I have some issues I need to work through. I can't really do that around here—it's too noisy all the time. I just need some space so I can think clearly." Without giving a chance for anyone to ask questions, Andy walked out of the kitchen, climbed into his truck, and drove away. He didn't plan to return.

Claire hadn't seen it coming and only later did she learn that the words "I need my space for a while" were not entirely truthful. Andy had been sharing "space" in a small apartment across town for several months with a divorced woman from work.

The kids assumed their dad was upset and was just going for a drive to calm down. But when Andy did not return, his children became frustrated, angry, and afraid. "Is Daddy coming home soon?" three-year-old Cody asked his mother almost continuously. "Is this the night that Daddy comes home to us?" But Daddy had no plans to come home. The young children struggled to understand Andy's perspective, fearing that somehow by being "too noisy" they had driven their father away. Andy filed for divorce. He did not seek custody of his three children. The children, ages 8, 5, and 3, were devastated by the loss of their father.

A wealth of evidence supports the growing conclusion that an intact, nuclear family, with a birth father and mother serving as role models and caregivers, offers children the most positive living environment in which to grow up. Study after study affirms that the separation and loss of the original family is highly damaging to the growth and development of children. Studies also confirm that children are negatively impacted by the trauma of divorce and the loss of their original family unit well into their adult years. These emotional issues often carry over into the partnerships they form with other adults. They are suspicious of marriage, afraid of losing what they love, less likely to commit, and more likely to try living together without getting married. They also have trouble with issues of trust and can be afraid to accept and value a positive relationship. And finally, they often believe that if they really love someone, they'll end up losing that person.

It is clear to those of us who study the family that keeping birth parents together in an intact, nuclear family is a giant step forward in the healthy growth and development of children. In a society consumed by providing economic security and financial benefits to its offspring, perhaps the greatest gift we can give is staying together to provide the children with attentive nurture and care. Earlier generations intuitively understood the benefits that children received by remaining in a nuclear family, perhaps because earlier generations were less self-absorbed and less involved in a consumer mindset. In a world of throwaway convenience items, we are in danger of viewing marriages and families as somehow temporary and disposable.

Highly fulfilled, mutually satisfied couples tell us that in some of the difficult seasons of their marriages they stayed together "for the sake of the kids." As Hannah explained, "We knew it was best for the children if we stayed together and tried to work it out. I think if we hadn't had our three boys, we would have separated and probably divorced. But neither of us was willing to make our sons suffer through that. We watched other couples split up—some of them in our own family circles —and we realized it wasn't a good choice, especially when kids are involved."

Whether by the presence of children or by God's grace, Hannah and David remained together and worked to keep their arguments and fighting private and out of earshot of their boys. Over time, as they listened to sermons and tapes about how to conduct a marriage, they gained the skills they needed to communicate better, to solve their conflicts without anger, and to move ahead in their relationship. It was not easy. For every step forward, there seemed to be a struggle with old issues or problems that seemed permanent and unsolvable.

Today David is grateful that having children in the home caused them to work harder to remain together. Without the children, David fears the marriage would have ended badly. "I would have walked," David confessed. "I was tired of fighting and exhausted by all the stress. I'm one of those people who just likes for everyone to get along. I was ready to hit the highway, literally, and start over somewhere else."

Instead, David and Hannah remained committed for the sake of their kids, even when their affection waned and the tensions increased. Today, with refreshing candor and relaxed laughter, David and Hannah report a high degree of happiness in their married lives. They nurture other couples at their church but haven't yet admitted to their own children how deeply they once struggled.

"The kids don't know how close we came to splitting up," David admits. "And we don't have any plans to tell them unless, God forbid, one of them ends up in an unhappy marriage, especially if there are children involved. If that happens, I'm going to sit down with my grown son and explain that his mom and I almost called it quits in our marriage. I'm going to tell him, ask him, beg him if I have to, to stay with his wife for the sake of the children.

"We just kept thinking of the kids, and somehow we made it. There isn't any magic in that, no formula really—we just kept hanging on, and things got better as we kept trying. Every time I look at my boys today, I think how grateful I am that their mom and I managed to stay together and preserve the family that my sons are growing up in. We weren't perfect, but we kept it together."

6. Commitment to honoring your spouse above all other relationships.

We've known Merrill for perhaps 30 years. We've traveled with him, laughed with him, grieved with him. Merrill is one of our best friends. In all these years of friendship, we've never heard Merrill speak even one negative word about his wife, Nancy—not in public, not in private, not sideways as a "joke" in the moment, and not directly as a complaint. Merrill honors his wife.

While other couples may not manage to match Merrill's

record, the happy and satisfied couples we know often tell us about their commitment to honor and show respect to each other. When we think about honoring and respecting a partner, our thoughts turn to Merrill's three decades of marriage. First and foremost, Merrill's positive speaking has strengthened the core of his marriage relationship with Nancy. He has expressed his love for her by telling others that Nancy is a great wife and mother and a wonderful life partner. Nancy can relax within the relationship, knowing that she can trust her husband to build her up when he is with his church friends, coworkers, or relatives.

Nancy has learned, not from a verbal promise but by observing Merrill's behavior, that her reputation is safe with him. She doesn't need to worry about what her husband might be saying behind her back. When we asked her if she considered herself a perfect person, she laughed aloud. "Perfect?" she sputtered. "Puh—lease! I'm not even close. I listen to Merrill talking about me sometimes, and I think, *Who is he talking about?* It took me awhile, but I finally realized that Merrill is telling the truth as he sees it. He truly does see me as some kind of wonderful person. You know what? I think, over time, I've become more like the person Merrill always says I am. In a way, I think I've tried to live up to that crazy opinion he has of me. I wonder if I'm a better person today because of the way Merrill has talked about me all these years."

Have Merrill's positive words helped Nancy mature, grow, and thrive? Has Merrill's respect for her actually caused her to become a better person? Perhaps her perceptive question hints at a way all of us can help each other grow.

Marriage partners have a unique vantage point from which to view the flaws and imperfections of their spouses. It's easy to find fault, point out problems, and tell others how challenging our spouses are. Yet Merrill has chosen another way, a path that involves honoring and respecting Nancy so that others will also honor and respect her.

We ask Merrill if his speaking about Nancy was intended to give her a higher or better reputation among other people. Merrill shrugged his shoulders. "What I do is tell it like it is," he insisted. "Nancy is an amazing person, and I'm a lucky—make that a *blessed*—guy to be married to her. But, yes, I do believe that when I speak to other people about my wife, they're going to be affected by what I say. If I say, 'Nancy is hard to live with,' they're going to believe me, at least at some level. They're going to have less respect for Nancy than they might have otherwise. I want people to respect Nancy the way I do. I want people to get to know the amazing woman I live with. I've never tried to say she was perfect, although frankly that's how I see her. Instead, I've just tried to always point out her good qualities—the good things about who she is."

Highly satisfied couples honor and respect each other. Merrill and Nancy are a living example of how that works. Not surprisingly, Merrill and Nancy have one of the closest, most intimate, and most romantic and fulfilling marriages of any couple we know. No longer young, they seem closer and more loving than couples half their age. Much of the time they act like newlyweds, right down to the physical displays of affection. Is this because they each got lucky and found a good match, or is it because their honor and respect for one another have built a foundation of safety and strength, allowing their marriage relationship to grow, prosper, and flourish? It's a question well worth considering.

7. A commitment to serving your partner instead of gratifying yourself.

Happily married couples often tell us about their commitment to meeting the other person's needs rather than worrying about their own wants. For these couples, the death to self has become the life of a healthy and fulfilling marriage.

One of the most destructive attitudes that can creep into

any relationship, including a marriage, is the sense of *What's in it for me?* or *What about my needs?* Self-pity is a pervasive and evil monster. Whether this monster is lurking under the bed or elsewhere living front and center in the marriage relationship, it needs to be faced by partners who are determined to be rid of it. Like the seemingly indestructible creatures of low-budget horror films, the monster of self-pity may have many lives, popping up again just when you think you've finally beaten it. Don't give up. Keep trying.

Highly satisfied marriage partners told us over and over again, "It's not about *me*. Making a marriage work is about serving your spouse rather than worrying about whether or not your spouse is serving you." Sandra is one of many who told us how this really works. "I went through a time in my marriage when I felt that my needs weren't being met. Chris was wrapped up in his work, I was at home taking care of two kids, and it seemed like we were growing farther and farther apart. I wasn't happy. The kids were driving me crazy, even though I loved them. Chris would come home from work, but he would bring work home with him. Almost as soon as he walked in the door, I would lose him to the computer or the television. It seemed to me as if he wasn't helping with the kids. It also seemed as if he had lost interest in me as a woman. Our sex life had dwindled to pretty much nonexistent. I was getting pretty frustrated."

We asked Sandra what changed. "I'm not the kind of person to go to a counselor," Sandra admitted. "I mean, that's just not for me. I'm sure it's really helpful, but I'm not the type to sit there and explore my childhood or whatever. I was picking up my daughter from the nursery at church one day, and I saw Billie, an older married woman from our church. Something inside me just told me I needed to talk to her and tell her how I was doing. Billie suggested I give her a call. I called her later that week, and she invited me to come over and visit with her.

"That visit changed my marriage. Billie sat and listened to me and just kept nodding her head. She had the most sympathetic eyes and the most caring presence. I felt as if I could say anything to her and she would listen and care. I don't know how long we talked, but I told her about how ignored I was feeling, how our sex life was suffering. I mean, I told her the deep things about my marriage and how unhappy I was. Finally I was done. I had talked it all out. I had nothing left to say. Billie just sat there for a while, sipping on a cup of coffee, not saying anything.

"Then she looked straight at me, smiled, and said, 'Honey, if you want this marriage to get better, it's up to you and nobody else. The best thing you can do is be a good mother to those kids of yours and be a great wife to your husband. Instead of worrying about yourself, you need to forget about yourself.' I was totally shocked. I had expected her to say how sorry she was that I was going through all this. I thought she would give me a lot of sympathy and understanding. Instead, she was smiling at me and telling me to forget about myself and serve my kids and my man."

"I want to tell you something," Sandra said. "That was the most important and helpful thing anybody ever said to me. Nothing I ever heard was so right-on as Billie's words that day. She was right! To be happy in my marriage, I needed to quit being so selfish. I need to serve my husband, serve my kids, and be the best mom and the best wife I could possibly be.

"Here's what has changed for me since that day: absolutely everything. The kids are older, but they have problems as normal kids do. In fact, I wish I had more time to spend with them, not less. Chris is starting to figure out that he's been too plugged in to his job, not investing enough time in his family. He works fewer hours and brings less work home. He's become a much better and more involved father.

"I had two close friends in high school, and both of them

are divorced. I look around at the people I know, and I just start counting my blessings. I'm married to a wonderful guy who is faithful to me. He's a good father to his children. I see how hard he tries to balance everything and make it work. I look at him some days and I think, *Why was I ever unhappy? Why did I let myself get so dissatisfied with life?* I don't know whether Chris has changed more or I have, but both of us have changed a lot since those early days in our marriage.

"People say that marriage is hard work, but it really isn't. The hard thing is admitting how selfish you are and then trying to change, to stop drowning in self-pity, to look around and figure out who needs help and then to help them instead of whining. The most important thing I've ever learned about marriage was told to me by a 70-year-old woman. She told me to quit feeling sorry for myself and start being a better wife and mother. I'm not an expert on marriage or anything, but I'll tell you what I do know—Billie was right."

The marriage relationship between a man and a woman is the most delightful and challenging partnership in life. Successful marriages, ones that bring the greatest satisfaction to both parties, are based upon joint, significant commitments to God and each other. When these commitments are honored by both parties, God blesses that relationship, and the rewards are eternal.

David and Lisa Frisbie have been co-executive directors of The Center for Marriage & Family Studies in Del Mar, California, since 1982. Their biblically based ministry of encouragement and training for couples and families has taken them throughout North America and to more than 20 other nations.

The Frisbies have coauthored *Moving Forward After Divorce* and *Happily Remarried*, which deal with marriage and family issues, divorce, and remarriage. Using many examples from real life, they speak and write with hope and humor about the challenges of the marriage relationship.

Books include *Moving Forward After Divorce* and *Happily Remarried* (Harvest House Publishers)

3 Communication 101
DON HARVEY

I KNEW KENNY AND SUZETTE'S PROBLEM had something to do with communication, because on the client information form they both listed, "We're having problems communicating in our marriage." My only previous contact with the couple had been a telephone conversation with Kenny to set up the appointment. So this was my first face-to-face encounter.

What an experience! Kenny was a huge man. He literally filled the doorway. And though you always need to be careful about making snap judgments, I could see that just by his sheer size Kenny might be perceived as menacing. Contrast this with Suzette, who was as demure in stature as Kenny was mammoth.

Communication problems—hmm. Kenny worked in a business where interpersonal aggressiveness was well rewarded. Did this carry over into his marriage as well? Could there be a power issue here? Perhaps Kenny's argumentative, intimidating, or forceful nature had brought them to counseling. It was easy to make this creative leap—or at least consider it as a possibility. Yet as their story unfolded, my initial assumptions were contradicted.

The emotions driving Kenny and Suzette to come for a counseling session were vastly different, and to a great extent these differences reflected how each saw the marital journey. Suzette was anxious and concerned. "Scared" might be a better word—not of Kenny but for their relationship. She was determined to work on whatever problems might emerge from the therapy session. She said, "I know Kenny's not happy, but I'm optimistic. Coming here is the first step. I know we can fix anything that has gone wrong."

Kenny, on the other had, did not appear to be as optimistic. In fact, as the session progressed, it became clear that he was feeling hopeless and doubtful that anything could be done to help their relationship. Kenny confessed he had been unhappy since the beginning of their marriage—something he had kept a secret. Extremely sensitive to personal rejection, he had avoided conflict with a passion. He had never shared his fear of rejection or discontent with Suzette. So for years, whenever he became frustrated, hurt, or disappointed with something Suzette did or failed to do, he kept it to himself. The result was predictable. First, nothing got resolved between them. And second, Kenny became more and more angry and dissatisfied. With time, Kenny's anger turned to resentment, a common reaction. In fact, I define resentment as anger with a history. And that was where he was now—resentful.

Before this first session, Suzette did not have a clue to Kenny's real feelings. She realized he was distant at times, but she was unable to read his mind and had just chalked it up to moodiness. The degree and longstanding nature of Kenny's unhappiness was news to her. In frustration she confronted him: "I didn't know you were this unhappy. Why didn't you tell me? What really frustrates me is that I didn't even have a chance to deal with any of this. We didn't have to get to this point. You could have talked to me about it."

Suzette's words were sad but very true. It didn't have to get to this point. Two reasonable, bright, articulate, and well-educated adults should have been able to deal with and resolve the difficulties that naturally arise in a relationship. But they clearly had a dilemma. They now found themselves in therapy with separate goals. Suzette had come to work on the marriage and restore their relationship. Her desire was to regain Kenny's affection and to once again count in his life. Kenny had come to bring closure. He was hopeless—and he was through.

We're having problems communicating!

It's always interesting to see communication problems listed as a reason for seeking counseling. It can mean so many different things. Sometimes it means the couple argues a lot and has a communication style characterized by piercing words and slinging verbal barbs. Therefore, issues rarely get resolved. Sometimes it means the relationship is punctuated by silence and drama. The cold shoulder treatment or a piercing look is all the communication there is. And sometimes it can be much more subtle than either of these two scenarios. A subtle yet deadly communication failure would be the best description for Kenny and Suzette. Their communication problems were more of what wasn't being said than what was. They were cordial—even cooperative. Who would have suspected that anything was wrong? Obviously not Suzette. But something *was* wrong—desperately wrong. Kenny and Suzette's marriage was in crisis. Although it was crisis that had brought them to therapy, it was poor communication that brought them to crisis.

Kenny and Suzette had come by their communication styles honestly, just like you and me. An old adage says that an apple doesn't fall far from the tree it grows on. We get many of our traits and habits from our parents, whether learned through observation or passed on through their genes. I think there's some truth to the apples and trees adage, but learning is a little more complex than the proverb suggests. We also learn by what I call *surviving home*. Living in the milieu of our families tends to bring comfort and security to our lives. I call this a crucible experience. It's different from simply modeling the behavior of our parents. Crucible learning is how Kenny learned to avoid conflict. His mother was a strong and domineering woman. As a single parent of three boys, she had to be. She expected her sons to behave responsibly. If they didn't, things got intense. Kenny watched as his older brothers challenged their mother's authority, each vying for control. He detested the feeling this type of battling caused. It was much like living in a war zone. So rather than following in their footsteps, he learned what he considered to be a better way: go along to get along. Kenny found that it was safer not to buck the system. He reasoned if he could stay out of the line of fire and not create problems, things would go better. He also learned that if he would just put up with situations, eventually everything would calm down.

You're probably wondering why Kenny continued to behave this way even after he left home. Well, take a minute to look in the mirror. You're most likely doing the same thing. We all do. When we're at home, we learn to survive home. And when we become adults, we just replicate in our adult relationships what seemed to work for us at home. These patterns, habits, sensitivities, and tendencies stick with us. It's like tying an elephant to a stake. We've all seen pictures of a huge elephant tied to a stake and wondered why an animal that big couldn't just pull the stake out of the ground and walk off. Well, it could. It just doesn't realize it can. You see, ever since the big elephant was a little elephant, it has been tied to a stake. When the elephant-handler first started the practice, the animal was too small and weak to pull away. Even though it eventually grew strong enough to break free, it had spent so many years learning that it couldn't that the perception stuck.

In a similar way, Kenny's avoidance of conflict had become a learned behavior. Although he was older, stronger, and clearly now had other options, it didn't feel that way to him. His behavior was engrained. And we can all attest to the difficulty of giving up an engrained habit or lifestyle. Change for Kenny would require time and a great deal of effort.

Communication: What's that?

Several years ago, Jack Annon created what he called the PLISSIT model. His model suggests that each of us can be placed at one of four levels of functioning based on how we behave and on what is required to bring change to our behavior. I have adjusted his model to make it more applicable to a marriage relationship in general and, for the purpose of this chapter, communication specifically.

Level 1: Permission-giving (P). Couples at the permission-giving level are able to change their relationships by simply being given permission to do so. For example, some couples experience communication problems simply because they fear it may lead to a disagreement. They incorrectly believe having a disagreement might indicate something negative about the relationship. These couples need to understand that conflict is a normal part of being in a relationship. Learning to resolve issues actually draws them closer together and gives these couples permission to deal honestly with each other. This in turn frees them to better communicate and changes how they relate to one another.

Level 2: Limited Information (LI). Other couples need a little more help in order to bring change. They will require some limited information. For example, rather than simply giving them permission to have disagreements, some couples need more clarification, such as—

- Identifying avoidant behavior (What's being avoided?)
- Providing a thorough description of the various ways to avoid dealing with issues (How is it being avoided?)
- Identifying and clarifying the different reasons one or both of the individuals may be avoiding problems (Why is it being avoided?)
- Spelling out the consequences for the relationship if they don't change their ways
- Teaching what good communication looks like

Armed with this new understanding, couples are ready to deal with issues differently and more productively.

Level 3: Specific Information (SI). Some couples have simply never learned how to communicate effectively. These couples need more specific information or assistance in developing these important skills. Skills training can be gained through reading specific instructional material, attending seminars, or actually participating in training activities. Seeking good preengagement and premarital counseling is invaluable and should offer a skills-based segment built into the experience.

Level 4: Individual/Couple Therapy (IT). Some individuals or couples have some kind of issue, either individually or relationally, that will require outside help. For example, Kenny brought to his marriage sensitivity to rejection so keen that even though he knew dealing with his issue was best for the relationship, he still avoided doing so. Sometimes unhealthy relational issues develop within the marriage. These nonproductive relational patterns emerge over time and almost always carry with them significant, negative emotions such as bitterness or resentment. Because Kenny and Suzette possessed both nonproductive relational and unhealthy individual patterns, marital intervention would be required to change their behavior and resolve the negative emotions.

Most couples find themselves on Level 1, 2, or 3. They can take the information offered in this chapter, make adaptations to fit their relationship, and bring needed change to their personal or relational behavior. However, if like Kenny and Suzette you find yourself trapped in Level 4, you will probably need more that just information. As a couple, you need to seek the assistance of a qualified therapist. Because communication plays such a tremendous and pivotal role in the development of a successful relationship, it is absolutely vital for couples to make every effort necessary to gain the skills needed for good communication.

Communication at its best: speaking the truth in love.

Sometimes it helps to understand what something is by knowing what it isn't. With that in mind, let me ask the question "What is bad communication?" Couples participating in marriage retreats and seminars usually have a lot to say on that subject. "It's when your husband listens to you while he's also watching his favorite game on TV." Although some of us in the new millennium like to put a positive spin on this behavior by calling it "multitasking," it still makes for poor communication. "It's when your wife asks you a question, and before you have a chance to answer it, she tells you why what you're saying is wrong." "It's when your husband doesn't quite tell you everything, and later you find out the rest of the story. That's so misleading!" I could go on and on with these real-life examples, but you get the point. These examples of poor communication provide us with a mirror image of some crucial aspects of good communication, like giving attention, hearing, and honesty.

Paul's admonition to "[speak] the truth in love" (Eph. 4:15) not only sets a high standard by which to live but also summarizes much of what those who teach communication basics seem to identify as the key ingredients to good communication. Examining these good communication characteristics can help us understand how to speak the truth in love to those we care about.

Good communication is honest.

Many Christians would be offended by the mere suggestion they might be dishonest. However, when it comes to honesty in communication, many of us seem to err just about as much as those who do not claim to be Christians. I don't mean that we necessarily set out to intentionally and deliberately lie to a spouse, but neither are we completely truthful. Often not speaking the truth is done for well-intended reasons. We place a noble spin on it: "I didn't want to hurt his feelings" or "It will just upset her." We convince ourselves that nobility and kindness trump honesty. Yet not being completely truthful is a form of dishonesty. If honesty is an essential characteristic of good communication, then what effect does this form of dishonesty have on our relationships?

In my practice I have found that dishonesty takes two common forms: dishonesty with emotions and dishonesty with sharing of the complete truth.

Emotional honesty. People who are emotionally honest tell others how they really feel. "I'm sad, angry, hurt, frustrated, or confused." When we share our emotions and feelings, problems and issues can be resolved more easily and relationships become more intimate. Rather than talking to Suzette about how he was feeling, Kenny internalized his emotions and grew resentful. By not being honest, Kenny missed an opportunity to be understood and validated, and Suzette missed an opportunity get to know her husband. As a couple, they missed an opportunity to resolve negative feelings and draw closer as a couple. Reconciliation begins with honesty, and that means speaking the truth in love.

Being completely truthful. In frustration, Sherry shared, "John doesn't create elaborate fabrications. He just leaves important stuff out. He clearly doesn't grasp the concept of 'the truth, the whole truth, and nothing but the truth.' And because he doesn't get it, I can't trust him. Technically, John tells me the truth. I mean, he doesn't tell me anything that's false. So once again, he technically meets the 'nothing but the truth' criteria. It's with the 'whole truth' part of the formula he falls down. He omits things, important things, and he knows it. He intentionally misleads me, and that's why I can't trust him."

John truly didn't get it. He just shrugged his shoulders and admitted that he did leave out a detail or two, but it was just to protect Sherry. He didn't want her to get upset, worry, or whatever. His response to her distress was "But I'm not lying to you." In reality, John *was* being dishonest. Dishonesty is not limited to telling brazen lies. Anything that misleads or misrepresents reality can have devastating results to a relationship. The consequence for John and Sherry's relationship was emotional distancing. Simply stated, you can't draw close to someone you don't trust. If communication in marriage is not fully honest, it's flawed and misses the biblical standard. "Speak the truth," and you will be on the road to building a healthy relationship.

Good communication is loving and appropriate.

Virginia Satir, a noted family therapist, once defined healthy families as human beings treating each other humanely. That's not a bad thought. I believe that gets close to what Paul was saying when admonishing us to speak the truth in love. Not only must I speak the truth, but I also need to be concerned with how I do it, why I do it, and my attitude when I do it. Good communication must also be appropriate communication.

If I'm speaking the truth but my attitude is wrong—if I'm bitter or resentful or I want to hurt you because you've hurt me—then I'm not speaking in love. Rather than bringing you closer, this type of communication will only serve to push you farther apart. Your insistence that "I'm only telling you the truth" may be true, but it's the motivation or attitude in the telling of the truth that's creating the problem. If my goal in speaking the truth really isn't to bring resolution and bring us closer together but rather to debate with you, to win, to embarrass you, to discount what you're saying, or to control the conversation, then I'm missing the biblical mark. And last, if I'm speaking the truth in such a manner as to shut down communication because I'm being loud and argumentative or I'm using intimidating expressions and mannerisms, I'm not communicating in love.

In 1 Cor. 13 we get a glimpse of what loving communication looks like. There we find it described with terms like patience, longsuffering, not being puffed up, and not behaving rudely. This speaks a lot to the issues of how, why, and proper attitude. For communication between partners to be good, productive, constructive, and scriptural, it must not only be truthful but must also find its motivation in love.

Applying some communication nuts and bolts.

Communication involves so much more than words. It's reported that as much as 85 percent of what is transmitted in a conversation is nonverbal—an inflection in your voice, a look, a glance, a sigh, a rolling of the eyes. These cues support and enhance the words we use. This leads us to another aspect of good communication—congruence.

Congruence means there ought to be consistency between the words that are spoken and the other nonverbal expression cues that give meaning to the message. For example, if your partner asks if you want to go to a Mexican restaurant for dinner and you reply, "Sure," but follow the statement with a heavy sigh and a look of exasperation, you're sending a mixed message. Your lips may be saying yes, but everything else about you is saying no. This type of communication inconsistency (incongruence) will likely confuse your partner. This is where the biblical admonition of letting your yes be yes and your no be no (Matt. 5:37) may apply. Say what you mean, and mean what you say.

Feedback is another essential part of good communication. Jan and I have a water feature in the backyard: a large pot with a bubbler (a ceramic pot out of which water flows). We left it out this winter thinking the water in it might not freeze if we kept it continually flowing. Wrong! The water *did* freeze, and the pot cracked. So we toyed with whether to repair or replace it. We decided to replace the old one and bought another large pot. After a lot of discussion and feeling equal to the challenge, we decided to repair the old one anyway.

One morning as I was leaving the house, Jan asked me to place the repaired pot back on the bubbler. I replied, "I know—that's the same thing you asked me to do last night." The off-handed implication was that I was not so old that I was having memory problems and that I had heard her request the night before when she asked me to do it the first time. "And how was I to know that?" Jan asked.

What she was saying was that, though she had asked me the night before, I had failed to respond to her. She had no way of knowing if I had even heard her request. Because I'm an intro-vert, there are many dialogs that take place in my head but never seem to get to my mouth. I really thought I had respond-ed. However that response had not happened, and Jan was still looking for a simple acknowledgment that I had heard her message. Because I had failed to give her feedback, our com-munication was incomplete.

Feedback verifies that the message between the two parties is received and understood. The message really is incomplete until the sender knows he or she has been heard. Feedback may be something as simple as a visual nod of the head or a smile of acknowledgment. More often, however, it involves a little more than just acknowledgment. Good feedback confirms to the sender that the intended message is actually the received message. It confirms that what was said is what was heard and that what is being heard is actually what is being said. This could involve a simple restatement: "So you want me to use the old bubbler." Or it may involve a clarification: "Let me see if I'm hearing you correctly. Are you saying you want me to use the old bubbler and not the new one?"

Because so much of what we communicate is nonverbal, constantly utilizing a feedback loop may prevent misunder-standing and lead to discovery. Feedback between you and your spouse can be helpful in uncovering some underlying emotion: "I know we're talking about pots and bubblers, but it seems that something else might be going on here. Are you angry about something?"

Feedback loops can also help us deal with the inherent problem of each person having a different perspective. I refer to this as each partner viewing the other through a different set of lenses. When I say something to Jan, I have the advantage of knowing what I mean or intend to say. Knowing my own intentions, I give myself a lot of grace. I'm a nice guy. I don't mean to hurt her feelings. I'm not intentionally insensitive. However, Jan can't read my mind, so she doesn't know my intent. It's only natural for her to view what I'm saying through a different set of lenses, the ones that affect her. Therefore, not knowing my intent nor having the clarity that I have regarding what I mean to say can lead to misinterpretation.

To combat misunderstanding, good communication between spouses utilizes near-constant feedback. By learning to use feedback loops (such as acknowledging, restating, clarifying, questioning when you're confused, checking out possible inconsistencies), you'll find that misperceptions and misunderstandings can be avoided or reconciled.

Let's put communication under the microscope.

I firmly believe that we can talk our way to a successful marriage. I just as strongly believe we can talk (or not talk) our way to a troubled marriage. Having spent three decades working with couples of all ages, lengths of marriages, and at varying places in their relational development, I've been struck with the fact that when we communicate poorly, it's commonly done through one of two ways: (1) failing to deal or (2) failing to share.

Failing to deal: avoiding conflict

Kenny and Suzette are an example of a couple who failed

to deal with issues by refusing to face the negative emotions that arose in their relationship. Their difficulty was not in having conflict—rather, it was in failing to address it.

Conflict is a normal part of any intimate relationship. I don't care how much you love another person—there are going to be times when you do or say something, or fail to do or say something, that will cause hurt, frustration, or disappointment. It may be completely unintentional or the result of miscommunication, misinterpretation, or misperception. None of that really matters. Feelings are feelings, and until they're addressed, there's going to be tension in your relationship. So what are you going to do when this occurs? The answer to this question will determine whether your relationship moves in the direction that God has designed for marriage or not.

Couples have two basic choices when they have negative emotions; they can either deal with them or avoid them. There are consequences for both. Avoiding conflict means that problems and hurtful feelings will go unresolved. That is what Kenny did. You may think rationalizing your feelings away will make it better. This is what Suzette did by reasoning: "He didn't really mean to hurt my feelings like that. If I bring it up, it will just make him more upset." You may even believe that avoiding conflict is the Christian thing to do.

Regardless of the motivation or rationale you use to support your choice to avoid conflict, it all leads to the same consequences: anger and resentment. Avoiding will only build an emotional wall instead of drawing you closer together—certainly not the goal of marriage.

On the other hand, dealing with conflict allows for the possibility of resolution. I know you're taking a risk and there are no guarantees. But I also know that if nothing is ventured, there will be no gains. It could be that you have tried to talk about something and it hasn't resulted in resolution. If that happens, you can always try something else or get some outside help. Remember: with resolution will come emotional intimacy, marital stability, and growth in your relationship. That doesn't seem like a bad deal to me. And it's certainly well worth the risk.

Failing to share: being intimacy avoidant.

The marriage relationship is profoundly complex, and it's important to recognize that a marital relationship always includes more that just communication issues. Even when communication problems are absent, there's always more going on that can bring a marriage to crisis.

John and Diane came to counseling having made some major choices regarding their marriage. Probably the most crucial choice was their determination to stay married. At one time neither was sure he or she wanted to stay married, but the couple had worked through that big decision on their own. Now it was time to deal with reconnecting emotionally.

Diane summed up her main concern this way: "John won't let me in." John had a tendency to be very private. He would talk with Diane about superficial things: work, kids, where they might go on vacation, what they wanted to do with the yard, and so on. He was an active, responsible, and functional part of the family, always doing his fair share of housework. But when it came to sharing the deep things in his life such as talking about his feelings, John was just not willing to communicate.

John had learned his method of communication—or non-communication—growing up. He had managed to survive home by keeping things to himself. He realized early in life that opening up emotionally could bring unpleasant experiences, especially from his critical dad. John learned that it was safer to hide his emotions so no one could use them against him. As is often the case, when John entered marriage, he just followed the survival strategy that worked for him when growing up at home. The consequence of his strategy was a safe but emotionally distant relationship with his wife. This strategy nearly ended his marriage in divorce.

Avoiding intimacy by failing to share personal feelings is not uncommon in marriage. I'm not referring to just the avoidance of expressing negative emotions (such as frustration, anger, and hurt). I'm also referring to avoiding positive emotions: talking about what makes you happy or sad; sharing the joys, the dreams, and the desires of your life; talking about what God has been saying to you and you to Him; talking about love, your fears, and your concerns.

Becoming emotionally intimate with your spouse by talking about deeply personal feelings is crucial for the growth of your marital relationship. Such disclosure invites your partner into your life. This kind of heart-deep sharing strengthens and deepens your marriage relationship, bringing closeness and connection.

A healthy marriage needs emotional connecting. Donald Joy made this clear in his book *Bonding: Relationships in the Image of God* when he described us as "bonding beings" and "created for intimacy." In a spiritual sense, this is what we were created to experience with God. On a human level, this is what we were designed to experience in marriage. You can help your marriage stay connected by sharing deeply and by inviting the most significant person *in* your life *into* your life.

Communication: an act of love.

In marriage, communication is about love. As you know, it's difficult to define love. On one end of the love continuum we might define it as a feeling, an emotion, or as indefinable, relational chemistry. On the other end we might prefer a more academic definition like that of Robert Sternberg. He suggests that love is comprised of three separate qualities: passion, intimacy, and commitment. I favor all of these definitions. Love is an emotion and it does have passion, intimacy, and commitment. I also believe that love has a profile.

When we are really in love there are things we do that communicate that love. That communication consistently says, "I love you—you're the most important person in the world to me." This communication is more than words—it's underscored by my activities and actions. This communication is lovingly honest and always seeks the best for the loved one. And even if anger and confrontation are present, there's always hope for a positive resolution and growing to a new level of trust and intimacy. These actions provide a profile, a predictable series of actions that express passion, intimacy, and commitment.

There's no human relationship in our lives where this kind of loving communication is more important than our marriages. And communication skills are not some inherited or deeply mystical secret—they can be learned. As Christians, we need to be reminded that we have one final and ultimate aid in our quest for effective communication with our mates: the presence of the Holy Spirit. He has promised to help us both all along the journey.

So whether you and your spouse are confronting issues of great importance or are sharing your vision of the future, remember that God is with you and that the risk of communicating honestly and completely with your mate is well worth the effort.

Resources

Annon, J. S. *Behavioral Treatment of Sexual Problems.* New York: Harper and Row Publishers, 1975.

Couple Communication Program, Littleton, Colorado, <www.couplecommunication.com>

Harvey, Donald. *The Drifting Marriage.* Grand Rapids: Fleming H. Revell Publishers, 1988.

———. *I Love You—Talk to Me!* Grand Rapids: Baker Book House, 1996.

———. *Love Decisions: A Dad Talks with His Daughter About Lasting Relationships.* Nashville: W. Publishing Group of Thomas Nelson Publishers, 2003. <www.harveytherapy.com>

————. *Love Secured: How to Prevent a Drifting Marriage*. Grand Rapids: Baker Book House, 1994.

————. *Talk Your Way to an Intimate Marriage*. Grand Rapids: Baker Book House, 2000.

Heitler, Susan. *The Power of Two*. Oakland, Calif.: New Harbinger Publications, 1997.

Joy, Donald. *Bonding: Relationships in the Image of God*. Nappance, Ind.: Evangel Publishing House, 1997.

Miller, Sherod, et al. *Connecting with Self and Others*. Littleton, Colo.: Interpersonal Communications Programs, 1988.

The New English Bible, 2nd Edition. Oxford, England: Oxford University Press, 1970.

Satir, Virginia. *Peoplemaking*. Palo Alto, Calif.: Science and Behavior Books, 1990.

Wright, H. Norman. *Communication: Key to Your Marriage. A Practical Guide to Creating a Happy, Fulfilling Relationship*. Ventura, Calif.: Regal Books, 2000.

Don Harvey has a Ph.D. in marriage and family therapy and maintains a private therapy practice in Nashville. For the past 13 years, he has been a professor of graduate psychology at Trevecca Nazarene University where he directs the graduate program for marriage and family therapy. Don is a frequent media guest and speaker at national professional conferences, has published over 10 books on marriage topics, conducts marriage enrichment experiences with his wife, Jan, and is a Marble Fellow with *Marble Retreat*, a ministry committed to offering Christ-centered, brief-intensive psychotherapy for clergy couples in crisis.

Books include: *The Drifting Marriage* (Fleming H. Revell), *When the One You Love Wants to Leave* (Revell), *Talk Your Way to an Intimate Marriage* (Revell), *Surviving Betrayal: Counseling an Adulterous Marriage* (Baker Books), *A Change of Heart: Restoring Hope in Marriage* (Ravens Ridge Books), *Love Decisions: A Dad Talks to His Daughter About Lasting Relationships* (W Publishing; division of Thomas Nelson).

4 The Road to Conflict Resolution

JAN M. HARVEY

JANET SAT WITH HER EYES FOCUSED ON THE FLOOR. Her husband, Chad, sat opposite her looking out the window, mindlessly clicking an ink pen. The room was filled with the tension between them. They had come in desperation, declaring, "We need help to repair our marriage." Both were angry and hurt; neither had kind words for the other. Married only eight months, they felt as if they were at the end of their rope. The issue was Chad's chronic lateness. An only child, he had been parented in a lax, permissive style in which his needs always came first. Janet, the oldest of four sisters, came from a home where organization and responsibility were necessary and expected.

"I can't believe him," Janet snapped as the session began. "Every time we have a commitment to go out with friends, I'm embarrassed. He acts as if everyone should be happy to wait on him to show up. I'm tired of making excuses for him. I'm tired of trying to get him to be on time. I'm tired of trying to explain how much this hurts me. He just doesn't care. I'm tired of feeling as if I'm his mother!"

"I'm tired too," Chad quickly said in defense. "I'm tired of being pushed all the time. I can't have a moment's peace without her telling me what's next on the schedule. She's driving me crazy!"

While still dating, they had discussed their feelings regarding being on time. Although Janet had recognized Chad's tendency to be late, she excused it in order to keep the peace.

Since Chad was never confronted with the significance of the problem, he happily went about business as usual.

After they were married, Janet began her plan to transform Chad into a more responsible person. She told him of her frustration with his being continually late, but it seemed he didn't listen to her concerns. When talking didn't work, Janet resorted to more covert methods. She began to lay out his clothes for him. She set the clocks ahead to trick him into hurrying. She even had friends tell him an earlier appointment time than what was reality. Chad did not receive Janet's covert actions well. He became angry. She became hurt. The blaming and finger-pointing escalated, becoming more and more destructive. Chad and Janet were soon experiencing their first major marital conflict.

Conflict and Marriage

This conflict, and others like it, are normal in a marriage. In any relationship, especially an intimate one, conflict is normal. Maybe I should say it again: conflict is normal. Recently, in a preengagement session a young woman said, "I'm beginning to understand that having arguments doesn't mean we aren't meant to be together. If our goal is to solve our problems, we can." Marital disagreement is the way in which one partner attempts to show the other that he or she is a person with unique thoughts and feelings. It is also an attempt to be understood, accepted, and respected.

In a healthy relationship, each individual and his or her ideas are to be heard and valued. The freedom to express thoughts and feelings to each other and have those feelings validated as significant is vital to the development of trust. The assurance that you can trust your spouse to value your thoughts and feelings is not only the cornerstone of the marriage—it's also the key to resolving conflicts.

So the questions are as follows:

- Can your partner trust you with his or her thoughts and feelings?
- Do you provide a safe environment in which your partner's concerns can be expressed?
- Do you care more about being right than about your mate's feelings?
- Do you realize that to make fun of or to devalue his or her feelings damages your partner's soul and most certainly the relationship?
- Can your partner trust you to listen to his or her concerns without becoming defensive?
- Does your partner know you value him or her even if you disagree?
- Do you understand that how you resolve conflicts will directly reflect on the success of your marriage?

If I could give you only one piece of advice, it would be this: *Learn to resolve conflict cooperatively.* Conflict resolution is a skill that can save heartache, hurt, and mortal injury to your marriage. Because it is a skill, it can be learned—like riding a bike. And like learning to ride a bike, it will take time and practice.

This chapter can help you learn the skill of conflict resolution. However, don't hesitate to get additional help from a pastor or Christian counselor if the conflict warrants it. Remember: conflict is normal, but research shows that the persistent avoidance of conflict is the number-one cause of divorce in this country. Read on.

Conflict: Why is it so hard?

There are different types and levels of conflict. If I asked you to think right now about the last conflict you had with a loved one, could you tell me what it was? Was it a fight, a disagreement, an impasse? How did you resolve it? Sometimes resolving a conflict is as simple as being heard and understood. Other times, resolution is much more difficult.

Dealing with conflict is not easy for most of us. We avoid it because we don't want to feel tense or risk losing the affection of the one we need to confront. We may avoid conflict because we didn't see conflict resolved successfully in our homes as children. Some of us never saw Mom and Dad argue. Oh, they did, but it took place behind closed doors. As a result, many of us don't have models or a successful pattern of conflict resolution to imitate in our relationships with our spouses. Many of us witnessed the pain and destruction unresolved conflict can bring and therefore avoid it at all costs—even to the point of denial.

A young man described his home life this way: "My dad was the unmovable rock, and we were like the water always flowing around him. We could never openly discuss a problem, so I learned how to manipulate him to get my needs met." Then he made this confession: "I don't want to bring this same pattern into my marriage."

How did your parents deal with conflict? Stop for a moment and identify the process. When there was conflict in the family, who did what? Was the conflict avoided? Was there anger and yelling? Did some individuals react passively and give in? Was there pouting and the quiet treatment?

Most likely, you—as a spouse—still expect and practice the same process. Even though it may not have worked well, it's familiar, and you know how to do it. But is it working in your marriage? The reality is that without successful resolution, conflict can destroy a couple's intimacy. Without positive resolution, effort that should be spent resolving an issue gets focused on avoidance. Therefore, it's crucial that couples learn to deal with marital conflict in a healthful way.

Conflict and Peace

The apostle Paul states that Christians are to live at peace: "If it is possible, as far as it depends on you, live at peace with everyone" (Rom. 12:18). However, sometimes we confuse peace with absence of conflict. We think bringing up a concern will upset our spouse, so we avoid or keep our frustrations inside, convincing ourselves that the issue is not important enough to disturb the peace. Eventually, over a period of years, we are left with dealing with so many unresolved conflicts that we become filled with anger and resentment. That is not peace.

God intended for us to live peacefully with others, especially with our mates. However, real peace is founded upon honesty. To live as a married couple and constantly reshape the truth to avoid conflict leads to frustration and marital misery. In simple and direct terms, the bedrock—the foundation of a solid relationship—is truthfulness. To live any other way is too much work and ultimately destructive.

Remember Janet and "chronically late" Chad? Although Janet recognized she had a problem with Chad, she failed to honestly share how embarrassing it was for her. Rather than risk hurting his feelings, she ignored the problem and became increasingly more frustrated. She also wrongly rationalized that when they married she would "fix" him by helping him overcome this problem.

Each person in an adult relationship must take responsibility for his or her own feelings and actions. Once Janet began to covertly "help" Chad with his lateness, she began treating him like a child. Chad rightly resented Janet's help. He entered the marriage as an adult, and now he felt like a manipulated child. As with all adults, Chad was responsible for participating in changing himself, and Janet had tried to take that responsibility away from him. If Janet had been honest and confronted Chad with her feelings, he would have had the opportunity to take responsibility for his attitude and actions.

Following are some guidelines to follow as you get on the road to conflict resolution.

Start out with a full tank.

Marriage is a journey. And a successful marriage, like a successful journey, includes planning, preparation, participation, and perseverance. Conflict in a marriage is just one aspect of the journey. You should plan on conflict in your marriage. Make the needed preparations for dealing with issues that arise. Be determined to work out your problems as a team. Proper preparation for conflict resolution in marriage requires three things: (1) unselfishness, (2) genuine love and respect for your mate, and (3) flexibility.

Before trying to resolve a conflict, realize that the *problem* is the problem—not your mate. When dealing with problems, each spouse must be willing to commit to the following:

- solving the problem without needing to be right
- taking personal responsibility for contributing to the problem
- actively participating in the problem's resolution
- staying focused on the problem and not being sidetracked by other issues.

Steve and Susan came to me for marriage counseling. When dealing with an issue, Steve would talk for a while. However, when it came to discussing any part he might have played in the problem, he would exhibit the traits of a person having a panic attack. He would close his eyes, wring his hands, run his fingers through his hair, stagger his breathing, swallow hard, and begin to turn red. It was quite a sight. Susan would immediately back away from the conversation and change the focus of the discussion in an attempt to help Steve out of his overwhelmed state.

After ruling out any real physical issues and learning that as an only child Steve was famous for his temper tantrums, I began to watch him closely. He was a very skilled manipulator. Through these episodes, Steve controlled everyone in his household. The whole family was afraid to talk about anything that would get Dad "stressed" and send him into one of his episodes. After several years of avoiding getting Dad stressed, the whole *family* was beginning to show the signs of stress.

After a few sessions, it became evident that Susan, his wife, was also participating in the problem. Steve's method of avoiding conflict was to act stressed in an extreme way, and Susan's role was to back off so Steve's episode would end. The long-term result was that both Susan and Steve no longer felt emotionally close.

Steve and Susan highlight an interesting fact about resolving conflict. When a couple successfully resolves an issue together, intimacy with each other immediately increases. Think of it: *intimacy always follows healthy resolution!* It's one of those "high five" moments when you both feel great. More important, you feel secure in your relationship. This security comes from knowing you and your spouse resolved one conflict; therefore, you can do it again, no matter how difficult the problem. You're a team just as God intended you to be. Mutually resolving a problem helps bond a couple, and that bonding is the foundation of trust and intimacy.

Don't exceed the speed limit.

Knowing when to address a problem—timing—is a critical part of successful conflict resolution. First, when you identify a problem, promptly notify your mate. Don't wait to see if the issue is still bothersome tomorrow. Deal with it today, in a kind and calm manner. Many problems can be resolved on the spot. The offender is often unaware that his or her behavior is problematic. By identifying the problem immediately, your spouse has the opportunity to (1) know you better, (2) apologize or explain his or her intent, and (3) change his or her behavior. Problem solved.

Second, consider your present ability to think or reason through what could be an emotional issue. When I'm sleepy, the world could be at war outside my door, and I wouldn't care. At that point I don't have the ability or the desire to get into a deep conversation. The rule regarding conversations at our house is nothing heavy after 10:00 P.M.

Third, don't try to resolve an issue when you're angry. When you're angry, your brain stops processing new information. Resist the urge to fight back. It's fine to simply state what happened from your perspective and to express your feelings. However, when anger is freshly stirred, it's advisable for both sides to call a temporary time-out. And this time-out needs to be respected. Next, you need to make an appointment with your spouse to discuss the issue in a more productive way. Here's how this process might go: "Honey, when you made that last statement, I felt hurt and belittled. I'm angry right now. I need to calm down before we discuss it. I love you, and I want us to deal with it, so could we talk about it before dinner?" This scenario states exactly how you feel, what the problem is, and when you plan to resolve it. It also helps relieve anxiety and diffuse some of your anger.

Let me say a little about anger. Anger is not a sin (Eph. 4:26). It's like a smoke alarm that lets you know when something is wrong and needs to be addressed. Anger is an emotional response that lets you know you've been hurt, frustrated, betrayed, or frightened. Usually one of these four causes is at the core of our anger. The ability to identify the issue that's at the root of your anger is a valuable skill, and it will help prevent further conflict. When you realize that you're becoming angry or behaving angrily, stop and think about why you feel anger. Are you hurt? Are you fearful?

The next step is to *state* your feelings: not scream, slam a door, throw gravel as you speed away in your car, or pout. To react physically instead of speaking makes us appear rather animalistic. Stating what you're feeling usually prevents other negative behavior from erupting.

Plan for a positive resolution, and don't rush the process. Allow yourselves 30 to 60 minutes to discuss the issue. Personally, some of our worst experiences at problem-solving have happened when we've been in the car and had a time limit. So we don't try to resolve anything on the way to church. An unresolved issue can hamper Bible study and worship. My husband and I had to agree either not to discuss problems on the drive to church or to attend a church that was an hour away. We opted for plan A.

Getting good directions.

Whether you're engaged, newly married, or married for many years, you're probably aware that your personality and your mate's personality will eventually clash—if they haven't already. I have good news! Whatever your conflict resolution patterns, it's not too late to learn to do it right. If you're early in your relationship, know that current problems are likely to stay with you for the duration of your marriage. Ignoring the problem or putting off the skills needed for conflict resolution is unadvisable. However, it's not unusual to see a couple's attitude change dramatically when they resolve a conflict together in counseling. It's a tremendous motivator and a great relief for a couple to realize that in one hour an issue that has been a huge problem can be resolved with mutual agreement.

After a counseling session with Chad and Janet, she observed, "Oh, you don't know how much this means to us. I was beginning to wonder if I had made a huge mistake in marrying Chad." Engaged couples often think they can get every issue resolved before they walk down the aisle. However, it's not uncommon for a couple to need help learning the tried-and-true steps to conflict resolution the first few times they face difficult issues. Ideally, these skills can be learned in premarital sessions. If not, don't delay in seeking out a pastor, counselor, or therapist who has been trained in conflict resolution. Let's look at the steps together.

Listen up. We all want and need to be heard and understood. Psychological research confirms that being understood by another is one of our greatest needs. A mature individual will make every effort to know and love his or her spouse. This includes both vulnerabilities and strengths. The kind of marriage in which a spouse feels loved and understood is also a marriage in which relational safety and intimacy have been nurtured. My guess is that half the arguments in marriage happen because the spouse with the issue doesn't feel that the other party has really understood his or her perspective. Therefore, intentional listening is vital in a marriage relationship.

In Chad and Janet's marriage, Chad had given up listening. Janet's role had degenerated into complaining, nagging, and manipulation. It didn't take many occasions of her nagging and complaining before he pulled out his mental earplugs. He heard her voice but stopped listening to what she was saying. While she spoke, Chad diverted his attention to other activities, such as the newspaper, the television set, or planning his next activity. He was miles away mentally.

You can be a *hearer* and not a *listener*. When you're a good listener, you listen for the heart-cry of your mate. You empathize and try to understand what he or she is really feeling. When we share our concerns and feelings, we're sharing our most private, unique, and special thoughts. If you make fun of your spouse's feelings or ideas, you can deeply wound his or her soul. You've just hung a sign around your neck that says, "Not safe for sharing!" Your mate will have difficulty trusting you again with his or her thoughts and feelings.

Emotions are unique. They're not right or wrong—they just *are*. Emotions are real for the person experiencing them. Never question your mate's feelings. Just accept, believe, and try to empathize.

Often when our mates tell us their concerns and how they feel, we begin to plan our rebuttals and stop listening. When we're really listening to understand, we ask ourselves what's *right* about what our mate is saying. A good listening practice is to repeat back to your mate exactly what you've heard, including his or her feelings on the subject. Then validate the feelings that were shared by your spouse. Tell him or her that you can understand why he or she would feel that way. Even if you disagree with the position, you can always validate the feelings. Validating is important because it says, "I love you, understand you, and value you." This level of listening makes the speaker feel heard. When this happens—and not before—you're ready to begin resolving the issue.

Speak up. A major contributor to the problem between Chad and Janet was that she had never expressed to him in a nonthreatening way how she really felt about his habit of being late. The spouse with the issue must learn to be assertive. Assertiveness does not mean being pushy or demanding. It means that you say what you *want or need* to say clearly and briefly, with kindness and respect. Don't be vague. Learn to use "I" statements and avoid "you" statements that put your spouse on the defensive.

In addition to stating your needs, state how you feel when your needs are met. Some people, especially males, have difficulty with this step because they're not as experienced in expressing their emotions verbally. Say, for example, "I feel disappointed that we aren't able to go out tonight." When you preface a statement with "like" or "that," you've stated a thought —not a feeling. For example, "You didn't warn me *that* we weren't going out tonight." This skill often takes some practice, because we're accustomed to talking about what we think and calling it what we feel.

When learning this skill of communication, it's important not to interrupt our spouses by talking over them. Stating your need while they're stating theirs will not result in greater understanding. Instead, wait your turn, and then state your need.

Insert how you feel when that need is met. Give an example as needed, and keep to a few simple sentences. In short, think of communicating in bite-sized pieces rather than a seven-course meal. Your listener can process only a certain amount of information at one time. I counseled a young lady who was very outgoing and talkative. Learning to communicate well in a few words was very difficult for her. It wasn't until I limited her to 10 seconds of presentation that she caught on and began thinking her statements through before she spoke. However, she learned to do it and do it well.

Be positive. Strive to make statements in a positive manner. For example, "I would like it if you would consult me before planning weekend trips with the guys. I feel secure and proud to be your wife when I see you being considerate of my feelings." The negative would be "You're always planning weekend trips with your friends without consulting me. Don't you think I have feelings and plans too?" Learning to state your concerns and feelings positively keeps you out of attack mode and makes listening much easier.

Stay on track. Couples must beware of negative behaviors that become a barrier to productive sharing by sparking anger. These behaviors are criticism, blame, accusation, and hostility. There's no place for these behaviors in the resolution process. Remember—your goal is to resolve, not to antagonize, hurt, or destroy.

Refrain from using sarcasm. Avoid interpreting what you think the other person is saying—for example: "Oh yeah—sure you're sorry. I know what you're really thinking." Stay away from answering with a question such as "Do you expect me to believe that?" These are all defensive behaviors that will prevent the sharing of information needed to understand and solve the problem. Some nonverbal behaviors such as rolling your eyes, sighing, and so on can have a negative effect upon fruitful communication as well.

Be proactive. State up front that you want to find a mutual solution. Say, "I know we'll work this out, and I love it when we do." Susan Heitler, a psychologist who specializes in conflict resolution, says there are three elements in collaborative resolution:

1. Mutual information sharing through respectful talking and listening.

2. A cooperative tone characterized by attitudes of mutual respect—devoid of criticism, blame, accusation, hostility, or antagonism. Negative elements in the problem situation are addressed without attacks on the other person; and

3. A win-win outcome responsive to all the concerns of both participants—rather than an outcome that yields a winner and a loser.

A win-win outcome should always be your goal. Sometimes you may think it's impossible, but it isn't. Positive, loving, affirming resolution requires that you address the concerns of both people. Just as the problem involves both of you, the solution needs to involve meeting the needs of both you and your spouse.

Pay attention to the "service engine soon" gauge.

Let's assume you've heard and understood your mate's concerns and feelings. Now, what exactly is the problem to be resolved? Usually the person with the problem will define the issue. If you're presenting the problem, do your best to clearly identify the issue. If you don't, you'll tend to bring up other issues and get sidetracked. I usually suggest that a couple write down the issue and refer back to it if they start to veer off course.

Let's look again at Janet and Chad. For Janet, Chad's habit of being chronically late was the issue. For Chad, the issue was that Janet was always pushing him to move faster, or creating a schedule for him. He felt he never had any time to relax. Both definitions were correct, but Janet was the one who was most upset. Therefore, we began with Chad hearing her concerns. As Janet learned to think through and verbalize what she felt and needed, she began to narrow the problem. "Chad, I need you to value me and our friends enough to be on time when we have planned engagements. When you do, I feel important to you, as if I'm really first in your life." Janet expressed herself well. She had assessed what her *real* need was and assertively stated it and then added her positive feelings.

Chad responded by telling Janet what he understood she was saying to him: "So when I'm on time you feel important to me? I didn't realize you were taking my lateness so personally. I don't want you to feel unimportant to me—you *are* first in my life."

I asked Chad what was right about what Janet said. He turned to her and for the first time validated her feelings. "Janet, I can see how you could feel that way. I've never thought about it that way. It wasn't my intent to make you feel unimportant."

Where did we make a wrong turn?

The next step is for each person to state what has been his or her role in contributing to the problem. Each person should be able to list two or three things he or she has done to perpetuate or keep the problem alive. Most commonly it's a behavior and an attitude. Taking personal responsibility for being part of the problem demonstrates humility and usually diffuses much of the anger. It also helps your partner be more willing to work with you toward a solution.

Chad stated he had been selfish in not caring about Janet's feelings and had not made being on time a priority. "I think I just tuned Janet's requests out and never actually admitted I had a problem." Janet admitted that she had nursed an angry attitude toward Chad and had taken on a parental role to try to change him. "I never really asked if we could sit down and talk about it. I never told him how I really felt." Each of them had contributed to keeping this problem growing. Hearing the other admit responsibility for the problem helped their attitudes so that they could work toward a solution.

Anticipate delays and detours.

After you both realize and take responsibility for the part you contributed to the problem, then it will be helpful to explore and analyze the techniques you've used in the past to resolve your problems. Then ask yourselves, "If it didn't work in the past, why keep trying it?" It's difficult to change our old patterns and habits. A good exercise is to write down what was tried before. Recording the unsuccessful attempts in detail helps you see more clearly how the previous efforts failed and can help prevent you from going there again.

Chad said, "Well, I tried to escape, spend more time at work, or go off by myself. I guess I just ignored Janet. Neither of those worked. She just got angrier." Janet also scrutinized her unsuccessful efforts: "I tried manipulating him every way I knew how. I set the clocks back. I had his friends call and set earlier times than we were supposed to meet them. I've nagged him and pushed him until he doesn't even want to be with me. I've taken the responsibility of changing him instead of really communicating my feeling to him." Both Chad and Janet were beginning to realize the predicament in which they had been living. They now were ready to solve the issue.

On the road again.

One of the three prerequisites for successful conflict resolution in marriage is flexibility. Here's the reason: creativity. Inflexible people do the same things the same way all the time. They can't seem to think outside the box. When you are creative, you allow yourself to be adjustable. You think of wild options and different ways to behave. It makes life fun. A creative person likes to brainstorm, saying or doing the first thing that comes to mind even if it's not practical. In fact, it may even be silly.

We all need a little humor in our lives. It makes issues seem less foreboding. When couples choose to lighten up, they can handle issues much easier. Humor makes what looked like a huge monster appear more like a stuffed animal.

Sit down with your spouse and brainstorm as many options as possible for a solution to the issue you're dealing with. Write them down and make your goal to come up with at least 10 ideas. The first few ideas tend to be the more practical ones, so keep going, and remember—be creative. Chad and Janet had difficulty with this task at first because they were so exhausted from dealing with the issue. But after they got a little nudge, they caught on and began listing their ideas.

They came up with 12 possible solutions, 3 of which were wild and crazy. Chad was beginning to let go of his need to be right, and Janet was feeling hopeful again. And they were working as a team for the first time. In their brainstorming, they addressed the issue of Chad being late and Janet constantly pressuring him. They listed everything from taping a clock to his head to scheduling some "Chad time" when Janet would not schedule or rush him. They talked about Janet leaving for events without him. Chad requested that she give him a one-time 15-minute reminder. They laughed and joked over their silly solutions and in the process came up with several good options.

Look for special roadside attractions.

Once you've brainstormed all the possibilities, you're ready as a couple to discuss which ones you will seriously consider. If either one of you thinks a solution is possible, it makes the consideration list. Once you mark the solutions to be considered, discuss the pros and cons of each option in solving the problem. Agree together upon which option to try first. Discuss in detail what each of you will do to make your solution a reality. It's important to be specific, and it helps to write it down. Both spouses need to agree that they'll give the chosen solution their best effort. If the option works, keep it. If it doesn't work, go to the next one on your list.

I usually advise couples to stick with an option for a few days and then evaluate how it's going. Couples often decide to try two or three of their options at once. No problem. That's great. The point is that you don't have to stay with only one option. Remember—you're flexible.

Let's look at our example of Janet and Chad. Janet and Chad decided to try two of their options. Together they decided on a time to leave for each engagement. Janet was going to stop reminding Chad of the time unless he asked her. If he wasn't ready to go at the appointed time, she would go ahead, and he would come later. She was going to be responsible for herself and allow Chad to feel responsible for himself. No nagging. Chad was going to set his own schedule and add in some private time. He was also going to set the meeting times with their friends for future activities. He planned to sit down with Janet for 15 minutes each day to discuss their feelings and progress.

Chad and Janet left the session in a much different frame of mind than when they arrived. Janet said, "You don't know what this means to me—to us. I know we can do this. I'm encouraged." Chad smiled and said, "You know, it's time I became a husband to Janet. I didn't realize how much my habit of being late affected her. I've been a pretty selfish person. Being an only child, I've always done what I wanted, and everyone was OK with that. It's time I grew up." They no longer felt attacked or defensive. They were taking personal responsibility for themselves and the future of their marriage relationship.

As a couple, don't be discouraged if none of your original ideas turn out to be a permanent solution. If both of you feel your concerns have been heard and addressed, you'll eventually experience the process as win-win and will be more open to trying similar solutions to problems in the future. What's important is that you've been collaborative instead of oppositional in working out a plan to solve your problem.

When you see your partner working on his or her part of the solution, make a special effort to acknowledge it and say thank you. Plan a celebration or special date to assess how your plan is working. You've done it, and you deserve it. You're a team.

Conclusion: Are we there yet?

Because a marriage brings together two special and unique persons from different backgrounds, there are some issues in your relationship on which you'll never agree. Ideally, those issues are minor and are not related to the values on which you base your life and your marriage. There are some issues in our marriage that Don and I pull out every so often. We're able to look at them again and reassess our individual positions. Sometimes we've changed our positions, and sometimes we haven't —but they're not issues that threaten our intimacy with one another. We feel we need to keep plugging along on some of the issues, and there are others we have mutually decided to not bring up. We can and do laugh at our individuality and even value each other for it.

If you're struggling as a couple to resolve your issues, seek outside help. No issue is insurmountable, but there are times a couple may need the help of a pastor or counselor. Don't be afraid to seek out a coach or a mature married couple who can help teach both of you how to navigate through conflict. Marriage is a great journey. Even with the bumps in the road, it's well worth the trip.

Resources

Godwin, Alan E. *Rules of Engagement: How to Fight Fair.* Nashville: Integrity Resources. Manuscript in press at this writing.

Heitler, Susan. *Conflict Resolution: Essential Skills for Couples and Their Counselors.* <www.therapyhelp.com>

Olsen, David. PREPARE Assessment Instrument. <www.prepare-enrich .com>

Jan M. Harvey is a marriage and family therapist specializing in preengagement, premarital, and marriage counseling. Jan is particularly interested in the preventative/psycho-educational side of therapy and enjoys relating with young adults. She also works with the Career and Counseling Center on the campus of Trevecca Nazarene University.

Jan and husband, Don, enjoy working together to strengthen Christian marriages and families. They regularly host marriage-focused weekend retreats throughout the country, are media guests, and are speakers for premarital workshops for colleges and universities. They also professionally give one month per year to Marble Retreat, a brief intensive counseling retreat center, specifically for clergy and lay couples, in Marble, Colorado (<www.marbleretreat.org>).

5 Managing Stress in Marriage

ROY ROTZ

MOST OF US RECALL THE DEVASTATING TSUNAMI that struck the Indian Ocean region the day after Christmas in 2004. We saw the mind-boggling pictures on the television news programs and read the stories about it in magazines. Just a few days ago I watched a documentary that focused on the tsunami. The most riveting part was a video someone took from a hill adjacent to the beach on an island in Thailand. English subtitles translated the conversation of the videographer, who remarked about the strange phenomenon occurring on the horizon. Again and again he repeated, "I have never experienced anything like this!" A blurry, white line far out at sea soon morphed into the giant wave that caused extensive damage and heartbreak. People continued to stroll mindlessly along the beach despite entreaties about the impending disaster from those who were on higher ground. Suddenly the wall of water moving at express-train speed struck ferociously, clearing the beach and wreaking havoc. The desolation that occurred with little or no warning was beyond description or comprehension.

In contrast, I've lived in the midwestern United States for the last several years, where we're often susceptible to drought and heat waves. Cool, mild spring days can descend into a sweltering, humid midsummer that renders a person completely devoid of energy and motivation. Most of the energy is spent running from one air-conditioned building to the next. Moving lethargically from one obligation to another is the rule of the day. Wishing for the cool, temperate days of late April and early May and wondering how the heat wave happened stay in the uppermost part of the mind.

Interestingly, these two very different climactic phenomena illustrate the two major types of stress in marital relationships. The tsunami is like acute stress or crisis that threatens to completely sweep away everything we assume to be stable. The summer heat wave is more like chronic stress that builds over time, leaving persons drained, listless, and longing for the refreshing breezes of a stress-free existence. The truth is—stress is a normal part of every relationship. As a practical matter, we must find ways to reduce it in order to manage it.

Webster defines stress simply as "mental or physical tension or strain." The clinical disciplines of psychiatry and psychology have developed elaborate descriptions about stress and equally complex theories about the best way to cope. Personally, I like the definition found on a button that someone gave me long ago: "Stress—the confusion created when one's mind overrides the body's basic desire to choke the living daylights out of some person who desperately needs it." Does this sound familiar? Have you ever been tempted to act on that? Whoever defined stress that way spoke for nearly all of us. It's a common and unavoidable experience. It happens in every area of life and can be especially noticeable in marriage. Idealistically, there may be a tendency to try to eliminate stress—but a more realistic goal is to manage it.

Stress and the Body

The physical impact of stress can be remarkable. Medical journals are filled with research documenting the correlation between high levels of stress and the breakdown of the body. A person becomes susceptible to heart disease, cancer, pulmonary problems, and chronic fatigue syndrome, just to name a few. In the 1930s Hans Selye pointed out the three stages a body goes through in adapting to stress. The first is what he called an alarm reaction, in which the blood pressure rises, the heart rate quickens, blood sugar goes up, and the adrenal gland dumps a load of adrenaline into one's system. Muscles tense, pupils dilate, and the breathing rate increases in preparation to deal with the stressor that's perceived. As Sherod Miller points out, it is "a mixture of alertness, anticipation, curiosity and fear."

The second stage is called resistance. The body's response to this stage is to begin to resist and adjust to the pressure generated by the stressor. It tries to restore the sense of balance. If a person's response is effective, the body returns to its normal functioning and "rests and restores itself" before engaging the next threat.

At those times when the response does not work, the stressor continues to be present, feelings stay very negative, and the person goes back to stage one—the very vigilant state. It takes enormous amounts of energy to maintain this hypersensitive state and places excessive strain on the body. In time, you may pass beyond the ability to physically adjust, and your body is unable to restore equilibrium. The third stage, exhaustion, then takes over, and chronic stress can lead to the suppression of the immune system, which can have serious long-term consequences.

Interestingly, low-grade stress can generally be noticed in the upper third of your body. Neck muscles become tense, which may lead to headaches. Your shoulders begin to roll up toward your ears. You breathe from the upper part of your lungs, through your mouth, resulting in an insufficient oxygen supply to your bloodstream that causes tiredness and fatigue. I've noticed this happening to me and have used that physical message to alert me to the level of distress. Consequently, I can choose to exercise some simple, physical stress relievers that help reduce the tension.

Simply sitting down and lowering your shoulders can help reduce stress. If you're standing, lower your shoulders, and let your arms hang loosely by your sides. If seated, let your shoulders relax by letting your elbows rest by your hipbones. Then close your mouth (with shoulders relaxed), and breathe deeply through your nose from your diaphragm. Take 10 deep breaths. Let your head droop down to your chest to relax the neck muscles. Allow your hands and arms to drop to your side. Progressively tense then relax the muscles in your body, starting from your feet and working upward. In just a few minutes you'll feel much better, less tense, and far less fatigued.

Sources of Internal Stress

The sources of stress fall into two basic categories: internal and external. Internal sources tend to revolve around how I perceive myself, including how capable I think I am and how I judge my actions toward others. The negative side of the self-perception is shame. The negative side of the second external sources—judging my actions toward others—is guilt. Unfortunately, far too many Christians struggle with elevated levels of internal distress because of a distorted perception of self. One of the most effective weapons Satan uses to keep good people stuck in bad places is shame. Harper and Hoopes define shame as "an emotion in response to a negative evaluation of one's self." They distinguish between shame and guilt by suggesting that guilt is "an evaluation of behavior." The difference lies in how a person sees *who* he or she is (shame) compared to how a person sees *what* he or she does (guilt).

Harper and Hoopes make the distinction even more clear. "Guilt is emotionally healthy and a necessary process of living with others, as long as it is an evaluation of behavior rather than being, leads to changing that behavior, and is not chronically excessive." Shame, on the other hand, pushes persons to "interpret every incident as validation of how worthless they are, how bad they are, how unlovable, how incapable of loving and giving to others. All shame-prone people also experience guilt; however, rather than being healthful, this guilt is excessive, chronic, intense, and rarely producing of a change in behavior." How skilled are you at telling the difference? Does the depiction of the "shame-prone person" sound familiar? Does it describe you or the one with whom you live?

Going back for a moment to the contrast between the tsunami and the heat wave, struggles with shame tend to be more like the heat wave. The distorted self-perception tends to become so ingrained that a person comes to regard it as normal and "just who I am." It's debilitating and draining, incredibly hard on the one seeing himself or herself that way, and equally hard on those with whom he or she lives. Being able to take responsibility for the wrong things we have done (guilt) is a wonderfully biblical way to help relieve internal distress. King David's confession, recorded in Ps. 51, is a marvelous example of the cleansing, relieving, motivating process that occurs when one confesses and repents.

When guilt is the problem, I can ask for and receive forgiveness as well as find myself in a position to grant forgiveness to one who has hurt me. However, when shame is the root issue, it's a different story. If I consistently see myself as fatally flawed, unworthy, and unlovable, I'll find it nearly impossible to find an objective position in which I'm able to take proper responsibility for my actions and confess what I've done. "See —I told you so!" is the distorted, internal message that shame brings. The shame tape plays over and over: "You're no good. You're stupid. You'll never get it right. It's no wonder things always turn out bad."

When I'm stuck in shame, I'll take a disproportionate share of the blame when something goes awry with my spouse. He or she may be responding to a guilt message in his or her own life and take appropriate responsibility for his or her share of the problem. He or she may even ask for or extend forgiveness, but because I'm stuck in shame, I'm unable to receive it. I feel undeserving of any relief, unworthy of that kind of love, and I believe that I'm doomed to remain mired in the "slough of despond" as Bunyan so eloquently wrote in *The Pilgrim's Progress*. I can respond to guilt by acknowledging and then adjusting what I do. It's far more difficult to deal with shame, because it's hard to change "who I am." That takes divine intervention.

There's hope for the shame-prone. Paul's words in 2 Cor. 5:17 are the clearest scriptural expression of the provision of Christ for redemption and reconciliation. "If anyone is in Christ, he is a new creation; the old has gone, the new has come!" In verse 21 of the same chapter, he reiterates the cleansing and empowering work of Christ on the Cross: "God made him who had no sin to be sin for us, so that in him we might become the righteousness of God." Through Christ, God has made it possible to be released not only from the burden of guilt but also from the stain of shame. He sees the forgiven sinner as a "new creation," not someone who is indelibly marred by sin and shame. The response of the shame-prone is one of gratitude for what the Lord provides, and equally important, a willingness to release the shame. If God has made me new from the inside out, who am I to continue to hold the shame He has released?

When the garbage man comes by my house each week, I simply put the stuff on the curb, and he faithfully carries it away. I don't wish to have it back. I don't follow the big truck to the landfill to see what will ultimately happen to it. I don't quiz the garbage man on his intentions or on his destination. I just put it on the street and forget it. That's what Christ wants each of us to do with our shame. Give it to Him, and allow Him to dispose of it. When Satan tempts you to return to the old habit of living with a distorted sense of self that's shame-prone, can you "bag it up" and set it out for the Lord to carry away? When you do, remind the devil that you've given your shame to Jesus, that you're a "new creation," and that Christ has carried it away and cancelled its power over your life. As the Lord releases you from the distortion and despair of shame, you'll find the ability to handle guilt appropriately, and the internal stressors will begin to dissipate.

External Sources of Stress

External sources of stress are the circumstances or events that occur for which one may be unprepared. The sudden things that happen to me over which I have little or no control, or perceive that I have no control over, can induce acute stress —the tsunami. Anyone who has experienced the shock of an unexpected death to a family member or loved one knows exactly how devastating it can be. If you've been unjustly fired from your employment, you've been caught in the tsunami. Having your spouse announce to you that he or she is leaving you for someone else brings on acute, painful distress that can drive one to despair. The most normal manner in which we respond to this tsunami is grief.

Elizabeth Kubler-Ross describes the five stages of grief that occur when one copes with any major loss:

- Denial
- Anger
- Bargaining
- Depression
- Acceptance

Let's briefly look at these stages more closely.

Denial is the emotional equivalent of going into physical shock. It's a numbing, surreal kind of sensation that leaves one with a weird sense of unreality. "I can't believe this is happening! Maybe I'll just wake up and this nightmare will be over." These statements are indicative of one who's in the first stage of grieving a loss. A person experiencing denial may continue to function for the short term, but it's only because the emotional pain is being anesthetized by denial.

Denial may give way to *anger* and bitterness. A strong reaction against the injustice of what is or has happened can flood one's heart and mind. Anger may be directed inwardly at one's own inability to make sense out of the incomprehensible. It's not uncommon for anger to be projected outwardly toward God, who is thought to be indifferent, or to a close member of the family or a friend who is trying to be helpful. In some cases involving death, it isn't unusual for anger to be directed toward the deceased loved one for having the audacity to die and leave the grief-stricken person in such a predicament.

The third stage of grieving, *bargaining*, arises when the anger begins to dissipate. "I'll be the best husband if my wife will be healed [returns to me, and so on]." Negotiating predominates in this stage of grief. The person is tempted to change anything about himself or herself to bring about a desired outcome. "I'll pray harder, have more faith, or witness more diligently if the adverse effects are altered.

The fourth stage of grieving comes about when bargaining begins to lose its impact and the individual realizes that all the "what ifs" and "if onlys" in the world would have made no difference in the outcome. *Depression* may begin to rule a person's life. A pervasive and all-encompassing sadness can paint the brightest relationship or the most positive response with a black brush. Clinical depression, characterized by significant changes in appetite, disruptions in sleep patterns, excessive irritability, difficulty in concentration and/or decision-making, may threaten the daily existence of one who has previously functioned quite effectively. The combination of good psychotherapy and effective antidepressants may help to relieve the low mood and lethargy resulting from depression.

Finally, one who grieves may come to the realization that things are always going to be different and life will never be the same. That's called *acceptance*. "I must learn to cope. I must find ways to acknowledge the new reality in which I find myself. I can't hide from the grief; I can't minimize it; I can't change and undo what happened"—these are all healthy signs of good grief. Talking about the loss, praying with someone about the difficulty of adjusting to it, helping someone who is going through a similar experience are all good ways to reach the healthy fifth stage of the grief cycle.

One can't expect to cleanly and surgically go through the first, then to the second, and so on. These stages have a tendency to get all mixed together at times. A person may be well into the third stage, bargaining or even be battling depression, and something will happen that sends him or her back into one of the earlier stages. In fact, a person may have gone all the way through the stages of grief when something will happen and the person is reminded of the tremendous loss that has been suffered and may go back to any or all of the preceding stages.

One of my college professors lost an eight-year-old son through a tragic drowning incident. By the time I was an undergraduate, the accident was 10 or 12 years in the past. My professor said it was very hard for him to see a group of third-grade boys walk down the neighborhood sidewalk, because they reminded him of his son. He would go back ever-so-briefly to some if not all of the stages.

- "I still can't believe . . ." (denial)
- "God, why did you let him die?" (anger)
- "I would give anything to have him back." (bargaining)
- "Will this ever be over?" (depression)
- "I miss him terribly, but as a Christian I'm aware that I'll see him again." (acceptance)

An equally important point is that it's possible to get stuck in morbid grief. This happens when the final stage (acceptance) is blocked. A person stays in a depressed state or fluctuates up and down the cycle without ever coming to acknowledge the changed reality of life beyond loss. One of the more dramatic symptoms is expressed in the morbid grief of parents who lost an adolescent daughter in a boating accident but rigidly insist on keeping her bedroom exactly and precisely the way it was the day she left on the trip. No one is allowed to go in, and absolutely no change is permitted for fear that her memory and existence will be forever erased.

Understanding that grieving is a normal way to respond when the tsunami strikes can lead one who suffers to move in a healthful way through to acceptance. It can also be an aid for one who wishes to be supportive and to help a grieving friend or spouse. Often it's not the words that are spoken but rather the presence of the comforter that's most critical. The Bible reminds us to simply weep with those who weep.

When a tsunami strikes your home, talk about it openly. Let your feelings be seen and felt. Identify the stage or stages of grief, and develop a sense of what might be expected next. Do these things empathically and without a trace of judgment. Listen carefully without hurrying to provide explanations or solutions. Sometimes simply being heard is the best medicine of all.

Our niece and her husband anticipated the birth of their second child, a little boy, just last summer. He was born on my wife's birthday, and because of the very close relationship that she and her niece Cindy have, Daniel Ray quickly became Renee's "birthday buddy." The pregnancy had not been easy, and the doctors were concerned about some health issues for Danny from the outset. Shortly after he was born, the medical staff told Cindy and her husband, Ray, that Danny would need corrective open-heart surgery at some point within his first year.

Danny was loved, cared for, and coddled by his parents, his sister, Emma, and grandparents, uncles, and aunts. He struggled to thrive in spite of the best efforts of family and doctors. The pediatric cardiologist decided to go ahead and operate in October, when Danny was just three months old. Ray and Cindy were told prior to the surgery that even for a tiny boy like

Danny, the operation was "routine," and the success rate was 95 percent.

Ray and Cindy waited anxiously at the hospital while surgeons began the procedure. What was scheduled to be a 6-hour surgery lengthened and stretched into 16 hours, and the anxiety throughout the entire support network of family and friends grew by the hour. Deep in the night, the tsunami struck as the surgeon informed the shocked parents that their little boy had died on the operating table. It is difficult to describe the emotional reactions that accompanied the devastating phone call from Idaho announcing the tragic news. Renee and I immediately flew to Idaho to do what we could to help.

What we saw from Ray and Cindy, the bereaved parents, was nothing short of heroic. Both of them have a strong faith in God and are authentic in how they express their humanity. They knew how to do what I have just described. Neither of them tried to minimize the force of the blow but engaged in a very open conversation with each other. Feelings were freely expressed, and no one discouraged their display. In the course of their conversations, especially with each other, Ray and Cindy talked and listened with deep empathy and a total lack of blame or accusation. There was no rush to try to explain the incomprehensible, no pressure to throw out saccharine solutions, but plenty of room was given and taken to grieve fully. The depth of their agony was shared undiluted with the Lord, and they acknowledged His gracious and loving response. In my opinion, they survived the power of the tsunami.

Chronic Stress

Enduring the heat wave is obviously different. The slow buildup of nagging, tiresome, never-ending kinds of things to which I find myself desensitized can lead to chronic stress. A job situation that constantly demands more than I can give, a toddler going through the terrible twos, a teenager who is struggling academically and socially, a husband who is preoccupied with ESPN, or a wife overly engrossed with scrapbooking are all examples of "heat wave" stress. None of these pose the imminent danger of the tsunami, but any one of them can prove to be draining and demoralizing if not properly addressed. If not managed, the heat wave can leach a relationship to the point that there's very little of worth left. A person can become acclimated enough to heat-wave stress that before he or she knows it, the marriage has dried up and blown away, and both husband and wife are surprised by how it all happened. To repeat Miller's point about exhaustion, for one in chronic stress there is simply no gas left in the tank.

Many times stress occurs in marriages at very predictable times. Whenever a life-cycle developmental change happens, stress results because of the differences before and after. Change is not easy, even if made in a positive direction. For example, the beginning of marriage, marked by the wedding day, is normally a very stressful time. The two individuals are in the process of figuring out how to merge bank accounts, homes, preferences, families, emotions, bodies, and a multitude of other things. This is all done under the microscope of a ritual that symbolizes the two becoming one. Another familiar life-cycle change comes with the birth of the first child. The entire dynamic changes, and much of the energy formerly invested in each other is now shifted toward a tiny, helpless infant who is unable to do much of anything except register distress at a very high decibel level. Research literature on marital satisfaction is consistently clear: marital satisfaction is generally highest in the early stages of the marriage and goes down dramatically with the introduction of children into the home. It stays low during the childrearing years. If it goes back up, it usually begins to happen after the last child is launched into independence.

Other examples of life-cycle developmental changes are when the first child starts school, when the last child starts school, when the children start puberty, when the first child finishes high school, when the last one graduates—and on the list goes. Add to that the other transitions that marriages must negotiate, and it's easy to see that stress is the result of some pretty normal things.

Fast-forwarding to the autumn years of marriage provides further examples of the life-cycle stages that bring stress. Having one or both spouses retire induces an incredibly stressful shift. With life expectancy increasing, it's not uncommon for a middle-aged couple to provide care for aging parents while simultaneously going through the process of supporting their young-adult offspring who are in the process of leaving the nest. Talk about pressure!

Marital Stress Symptoms and Solutions

When stress strikes in a marriage, signs and symptoms occur. One of the first is black or white thinking, all-or-nothing kinds of responses. Differences get placed in win/lose or right/wrong wrappings. Partners fail to objectively see *what* the problem is and defensively and subjectively fixate on *who* the problem is, or more specifically, "why I'm not the problem and you are." Global language characterized by statements like "you always . . ." or "you never . . ." may become the rule instead of the exception. Emotions override logic, and both husband and wife may become very reactive.

Just as the body prepares physically to deal with threat, we instinctively and effectively prepare to meet a threat whether real or perceived. Emotionally and relationally one may react in a "fight, flight, or freeze" mode. The fighter will attack and blame. The one who flees will withdraw into wounded silence. The frozen one just gets a deer-in-the-headlights look and a scrambled brain and doesn't seem to respond much at all. Since we each generally react differently, it's easy to see that stress can drive a painful wedge into even the most stable and resilient relationships.

Given that stress is normal in every relationship, is often predictable (heat wave), yet occasionally surprising (tsunami), what are some ways in which a person or couple can manage? I would like to propose a fairly simple method that could be useful to help cope with stress in your marriage. The "AAA method" might be easy to recall and helpful to follow:

Anticipate as many of the stressors as you reasonably can. This is not to suggest that you lay awake at night in dreadful fear of when a certain kind of stress will strike. It's to say that it makes sense to think ahead about where you are in your own life-cycle and what changes are just around the corner or in the process of occurring. This is like reading a map to some extent. The map is not the actual territory but is rather a depiction. However, you can look at the map and get a good idea of what's ahead in terms of twists and turns in the road, terrain, elevation, and sense of direction. Find time to share with your spouse the information you've acquired. Point out the hazards you see, and listen to your spouse's perception of what may threaten or where the road should lead. Then collaborate on choosing the best way to navigate through the rough place to one that's smoother and more manageable.

Renee and I love to ride our big Yamaha road bike. We have a trailer we pull for long trips. She rides behind me and serves as the navigator, or the "map-ologist," as we say in our house. In the summer of 2004 we rode nearly 3,000 miles through the mountains of central and western Colorado. We had a great time—with one significant exception. We started up Independence Pass to go over the Continental Divide from east to west, with the ultimate destination being Aspen. However, as we rode higher and higher, the road became more narrow, and the drop-offs were sheer—hundreds of feet to the bottom. I had been over this pass many times in cars, but never on a motorcycle. About two-thirds of the way up, vertigo kicked into high gear, and I started to get tunnel vision and hyperventilate. There was no place to turn around safely. I literally had to will myself to keep going until we made the summit and got down the other side.

We're getting ready to go on an even longer ride and will be traversing mountainous terrain again. We've spent lots of time poring over maps and checking information on the Internet, because we don't want to go through another situation like that. It's called *anticipation*.

Acknowledge the intensity and the degree of stress to each other. Don't bottle it up inside. Find productive ways to share the pressure that you experience without attacking or blaming. Can you tell if this is a heat wave (chronic stress) or a tsunami (crisis)? Is the source internal (shame or guilt) or external (situational and circumstantial)?

Sometimes the mere act of first identifying the kind of stress helps slow one down enough to think about a proactive response instead of a panic-stricken reaction to the pressure that occurs. Even in the face of an emergency, slowing down and keeping your head is far more productive than going to pieces and running in a more hazardous direction. Merely taking off into headlong flight is not sufficient. It's necessary to slow down long enough to see which way to run.

Acknowledge to the Lord the depth and degree of the stress you face. The Bible is clear that the Lord is present in every area of your life and will not leave you nor abandon you. Nothing that happens to you catches Him by surprise. He's able to help when the stress is chronic yet predictable like the heat wave. Psalm 119:105 reminds me that the word of the Lord is "a lamp to my feet and a light to my path." I may have an idea about what's around the next bend in the road, but God knows for sure, and He'll lead me. He has promised to provide for my needs (Phil. 4:19; Matt. 6:25-33). And He'll get *you* through the heat wave.

But what can I do about the tsunami? Listen to the words of the Psalmist:

I love the LORD, for he heard my voice; he heard my cry for mercy. Because he turned his ear to me, I will call on him as long as I live. The cords of death entangled me, the anguish of the grave came upon me; I was overcome by trouble and sorrow. Then I called on the name of the LORD: "O LORD, save me!" The LORD is gracious and righteous; our God is full of compassion. The Lord protects the simplehearted; when I was in great need, he saved me (*Ps. 116:1-6*).

Does that sound like someone threatened by the power of the tsunami? Yes. God will deliver in times of extreme stress.

One of my favorite stories is that of King Jehoshaphat when surrounded by an overwhelming enemy force. His people had no way out. Utter devastation and destruction loomed. The king frankly admitted the desperate plight in which he found himself and his people and prayed a very public and candid prayer. In my Bible I've underlined the portion of the verse that has helped me get through the tsunamis that have threatened my life. It is the last sentence of Jehoshaphat's prayer: "We do not know what to do, but our eyes are upon you" (2 Chron. 20:12). That is an honest acknowledgment of a tsunami-like situation where trust is placed in the only One who is bigger and more powerful than the wave.

Adjust by being willing to seek outside, objective help. It always amazes me how many couples come for help when the heat wave has already burned the relationship into desert barrenness. Equally tragic is when the tsunami is rolling in and the couple fights each other instead of finding a way to higher ground together. Both are destroyed in the process. Seeking professional counseling is not a sign of weakness, failure, or an indication of imminent doom. It's an admission that stress has overburdened the marital relationship and that help is needed.

Adjust by making a determination to stick together rather than letting stress "divide and conquer." It's very easy to allow all kinds of good things to intervene in relationships that could ultimately ruin them. Check the balance of where you spend your time and energy. How much is intentionally spent on the one who matters most to you? Are jobs, hobbies, kids, or church consuming more than what you have to give? Is your husband or wife getting the crumbs of what you have to offer while other projects or people take the loaf? Renee and I are very diligent about protecting time for just the two of us. I think that's one of the main reasons we've remained best friends for more than 35 years of married life.

Adjust by intentionally taking time to de-stress with regular time off. Do you have *and take* a day off? Many times I ask that question (especially of my pastor friends), and they tell me, "I have a day off." So I've learned to ask the second part of the question—"Do you *take* it?" Often the surprising answer is no.

Have you discovered fun, simple, and creative things to do together or with your kids? Talk to someone whose marriage you would like to copy, and get some ideas from them. Plan and take an annual vacation that's a positive memory-maker of the highest order. Taking off a week or two to paint the house, resod the yard, or move your mother-in-law to assisted living does not qualify! Get away from the chronic stressors of work, a home, and routine so they won't dry you and your marriage to powder.

For the tsunami, adjust by checking the horizon occasionally and listening to objective input—the voice of experienced peers or the voice of God speaking through His Holy Spirit. Look up once in a while to see what's on the horizon. Listen to the voices of experience around you to help you recognize danger signs in your marriage.

For the heat wave, adjust by paying attention to the little things to which you can become desensitized over time but could eventually demand a price that's difficult—if not impossible—to pay. Anticipate and acknowledge to yourself, to your spouse, and to your Lord. Then take the necessary corrective steps to manage stress.

It's a fact of life that stress is a constant in our lives and marriages. However, an equal truth is that we become stronger as individuals and marriage partners when we learn to rest in God and work with our spouses to address the inevitable stressing situations we experience.

References

Harper, James M., and Margaret H. Hoopes. *Uncovering Shame: An Approach Integrating Individuals and Their Family Systems.* New York: W.W. Norton & Co., 1990.

Kubler-Ross, Elizabeth. *On Death and Dying.* New York: Macmillan Publishing Co., 1969.

Miller, Sherod, et al. *Connecting with Self and Others.* Littleton, Colo.: Interpersonal Communication Programs, 1992.

Roy Rotz is currently serving as the associate academic dean for Graduate and Adult Studies at MidAmerica Nazarene University. He is a licensed clinical marriage and family therapist in Kansas and Missouri. He is an ordained elder in the Church of the Nazarene and has served churches in Oklahoma, Texas, Kansas, and Missouri. Dr. Rotz serves as a board member to a number of organizations that focus on family, marriage, and counseling. He has taught many advanced level courses in psychology, pastoral counseling, family, and marriage.

6 Building and Maintaining an Intimate Relationship

VICTOR M. PARACHIN

A LEGEND IS TOLD OF A YOUNG KING who married a lovely princess. Shortly after their wedding, it became necessary for the king to lead his army into battle. Upset at the thought of being separated from his new queen, he walked alone through the palace gardens for a time of reflection. Pausing by the pond, he tossed a pebble into the water and watched the ripple of circles form. *How like a circle is my love for my queen!* he thought. *No beginning and no end.* Inspired by the ripple of circles, he immediately called the royal goldsmith and asked him to make a gold circle to fit the queen's finger. When the ring was finished, the king slipped it onto his wife's finger, saying, "This circle, which has no beginning and no end, is a pledge, in my absence, of my endless, eternal love for you."

Ever since, husband and wives have exchanged rings as symbols of their love. Almost every couple who decides to marry does so with the highest of ideals and the most noble of desires. Yet the art of blending two lives, two personalities, two careers, and two perspectives can be challenging. Getting married is the easy part—remaining married and maintaining intimacy in ways that are mutually satisfying is a little more complex. Consider the following two descriptions of marriage, the first from a woman and the other from a man.

"When my husband and I started dating we couldn't wait to see each other. There was constant handholding, lengthy phone calls when we were apart, e-mails back and forth all day long, hugs and kisses upon greeting and departing. After we were married we were absolutely confident that our courtship pattern would continue and that we would not fall into the plight of reduced intimacy and desire so often described by many other married couples. Well, little by little, these things did creep into our relationship. Though there's no doubt we still love each other, the handholding, the hugs, the kisses, the phone calls, and the e-mails have become less frequent. Rather than lingering in bed on Saturday mornings, we started getting up early and heading off to the gym for a workout. Lately, I've been tormenting myself, wondering what this means and where we're headed as a couple."

"I'm not sure when or how it happened, but we used to be each other's best friend. When my wife and I were dating, she was the person I most wanted to be with. When I had a concern or a joy, she was the first person I talked to about it. We spent so much wonderful time talking, talking, talking. We asked questions, listened attentively, wanting to know everything about each other. After we got married, things began to change—very slowly, very subtly. We talked less, asked fewer questions about each other, fell into a rut, and, I guess, began to take each other for granted. At first the distance between us was hardly noticeable, but it continued to grow and widen. Now, while we're civil, we don't really communicate in depth and are seldom intimate. When we do talk, we complain more than we connect. I'm grieving the loss of friendship and intimacy we used to enjoy and am not sure how to regain those things."

These marital experiences are most unfortunate. Every couple will have differences of opinion and outlook and differences of intimacy expectations and needs from time to time. The good news is that these differences can be reconciled. Here are some key steps for building and maintaining intimacy. These steps can help overcome the distance that sometimes occurs in a marriage and restore mutual happiness and satisfaction as a couple.

Begin by understanding intimacy.

Look up the word "intimacy" in several dictionaries, and you will find descriptions such as "closeness; close or warm friendship; a feeling of belonging together; shared moments; feelings of closeness; knowing someone in depth; feeling understood, loved, appreciated; growing closer together." Intimacy is a basic ingredient in any meaningful and significant relationship. It is the basis of a sound friendship and foundational in a marital relationship. Intimacy is more than physical. In fact, a holistic and healthy, intimate relationship is made up of five aspects:

- *Intellectual intimacy:* the freedom and comfort to share your thoughts, ideas, and viewpoints with your partner knowing they will be heard and valued. It can mean anything from sharing insights gained from reading a book or reflection on the daily world news or an issue that came up at work.

- *Social intimacy:* spending time together and supporting each other's interests and life events. For example, she attends his Christmas office party even though she may not particularly enjoy her husband's colleagues. He attends the concert with her even though he might rather be home watching a sporting event on television. Another example: both are present at their children's athletic, musical, or cultural events. Social intimacies go a long way in developing a sense of teamwork.

- *Emotional intimacy:* sharing and being supportive of the feelings and emotions experienced by your mate. Your partner is concerned about her weight and begins a diet. You support her and perhaps even join her. Your husband, who has never considered himself athletic, wants to train for a marathon. Even though it's going to mean two- and three-hour training runs on weekends, you encourage him, because you know how important it is for him to develop his athletic side. The sharing and supporting of each other's emotional framework deepens and solidifies relationship intimacy.

- *Spiritual intimacy:* a level of understanding that prayer, Bible study, and worship are important activities that are supported by both partners. She is supportive if he participates in the church men's group, and he is supportive if she wants to be part of the choir. It's great if both partners participate in a Bible study together with others. The focus here is not necessarily agreement on every detail of belief and doctrine but that you both want to be growing spiritually.

- *Physical intimacy:* sexual intimacy is very important in marriage. However, for the physical to be meaningful and satisfying, the other four aspects of intimacy in the relationship need to be vibrant and vitally present.

Study and understand God's plan for marriage.

God intends for all of us to live meaningful, satisfying lives. In the Old Testament we read, "'I know the plans I have for you,' declares the LORD, 'plans to prosper you and not to harm you, plans to give you hope and a future'" (Jer. 29:11). In the New Testament Jesus says, "I have come that they may have life, and have it to the full" (John 10:10). Always operate on the assumption that God's intention for you as a couple is mutual fulfillment, satisfaction, harmony, and goodwill. Here are some biblical premises for marriage:

- *God made us interdependent.* "Woman is not independent of man, nor is man independent of woman. For as woman came from man, so also man is born of woman. But everything comes from God" (1 Cor. 11:11-12). We need each other and complete each other. "The LORD God said, 'It is not good for the man to be alone. I will make a helper suitable for him'" (Gen. 2:18).

- *Men are blessed by wives and are to please, honor, and love them.* "He who finds a wife finds what is good and receives favor from the LORD" (Prov. 18:22). "A wife of noble character who can find? She is worth far more than rubies. Her husband has full confidence in her and lacks nothing of value. She brings him good, not harm, all the days of her life" (Prov. 31:10-12). "Husbands . . . be considerate as you live with your wives" (1 Pet. 3:7). "Husbands, love your wives, just as Christ loved the church and gave himself up for her" (Eph. 5:25).

- *Women are blessed by husbands and are to please, honor, and love them.* "She speaks with wisdom, and faithful instruction is on her tongue. She watches over the affairs of her household and does not eat the bread of idleness. Her children arise and call her blessed; her husband also, and he praises her" (Prov. 31:26-28). "The wife must respect her husband" (Eph. 5:33).

- *Wives and husbands are to look after each other's best interests.* "Do nothing out of selfish ambition or vain conceit, but in humility consider others better than yourselves. Each of you should look not only to your own interests, but also to the interests of others" (Phil. 2:3-4). "Each one of you also must love his wife as he loves himself, and the wife must respect her husband" (Eph. 5:33). "Submit to one another out of reverence for Christ" (Eph. 5:21). "The husband should fulfill his marital duty to his wife, and likewise the wife to her husband. The wife's body does not belong to her alone but also to her husband. In the same way, the husband's body does not belong to him alone but also to his wife. Do not deprive each other except by mutual consent" (1 Cor. 7:3-5).

Remember that marriage is different from friendship.

Too many couples experience a disappointing decrease of sexual intimacy after marriage and don't take the necessary steps to make a correction. Left unattended, that void often creates dissatisfaction, distance, and vulnerability. That's why Shmuley Boteach, author of numerous books on marital relationships, tells couples to remember that marriage is different from friendship. He stresses the importance of sexual intimacy in marriage. He notes, "Sex is certainly not the only important thing in marriage. But it *is* what transforms a friendship into a marriage. You are not husband and wife when you simply share a home or apartment. That's called being roommates. Nor are you husband and wife when you merely share a bedroom. That can still be a platonic friendship. You are specifically husband and wife when you share the *same bed*, make love, and become *the same flesh.*"

Boteach laments the growing trend toward the "celibate marriage" and cautions couples to avoid that marital road. "A major trend in the United States is the celibate marriage. That is built on the idea that no marriage can really preserve its passion . . . just focus on the really important things, like going to art galleries together, discussing Vivaldi, listening to music, providing each other with comfort and security, baking lasagna, debating politics, and so on. *But these are activities you share with everybody else.* That's not marriage. Marriage is sharing one bed, and becoming orchestrated together emotionally and especially physically, as an indivisible unit."

Whenever you begin to experience an absence of such intimacy in your relationship, start by talking with your partner about it, and together explore ways of making improvements.

Upgrade your empathy skills.

Share your partner's emotions. Listen carefully to your

spouse's words and the feelings behind the words. Job pleaded with his friends, "Listen to me; I too will tell you what I know" (Job 32:10). Intimacy always involves someone talking and the other listening. Recent research from Harvard Medical School reveals that couples expressing the most empathy and affection are the most likely to stay together. Harville Hendrix, an author and marriage counselor, offers these tips for upgrading empathy skills:

- *Mirror.* When your partner expresses his or her feelings, show that you're listening by paraphrasing. Start with "Let me see if I've got that. You feel . . ."
- *Resist the urge to interrupt.* Instead of saying, "Are you through now?" try "Is there more to that?" Hendrix explains that this shows your partner that he or she can feel open and safe with you.
- *Validate your spouse's point of view.* Finish with "I can imagine that because of [fill in the issue], you feel angry [sad, guilty, and so on]."

The price tag for a lack of skill in being empathetic can be disastrously high. Repeated failure to listen and be empathetic results in a partner feeling uncared for and unloved. Lack of listening will quickly be interpreted as a sign of disrespect and disinterest. Consider the following unfortunate situation.

A man writing to an advice columnist outlined his painful experience. "My first wife and I got married right out of high school. She was the girl of my dreams, and I was ecstatic." Shortly after the wedding, the man inherited a family business that demanded a great deal of his time and emotional energy. "When my wife had a problem, I was frequently too tired to listen," he writes. "As that pattern of nonlistening continued, she gradually detached from the relationship. After six years of marriage, she found someone who made her feelings a priority. He took the time to listen to her." Sadly, the man and the girl of his dreams divorced. "I am now 28 and married for the second time. There are still times when I find myself reverting to old habits, but I know I must make the effort to hear what she has to say, or I'll lose her too." The lesson from that failed marriage: *upgrade your empathy skills; make time to listen; then listen carefully and respectfully to your partner.*

Kindness is a vital marital ingredient.

Romance blooms and blossoms when there are ample thoughtful acts demonstrating kindness and consideration toward your partner. If romance has been neglected or is absent in your relationship, begin immediately to restore it. Without daily kindnesses, marriages wither like plants that do not receive regular watering. That's why the Bible presents kindness as a supreme virtue in a spouse. In Gen. 24, Abraham is concerned about finding a good wife for his son Isaac. Abraham sends his trusted servant, Eliezer, to find Isaac a suitable partner. Eliezer leaves on his mission and offers this prayer: "O LORD, God of my master Abraham, give me success today" (Gen. 24:12). In addition, he asks God for a divine sign directing him to the right bride: "May it be that when I say to a girl, 'Please let down your jar that I may have a drink,' and she says, 'Drink, and I'll water your camels too'—let her be the one you have chosen for your servant Isaac'" (Gen. 12:14). Shortly after that prayer is offered, Rebecca arrives at the well and not only offers Eliezer water but gives water to the thirsty camels as well—a physically demanding task in that one camel can drink up to 20 gallons of water. The point of the story is this: kindness is the characteristic that distinguishes Rebecca. Seeing a thirsty stranger and his thirsty camels, she spontaneously acts to meet their needs. That ancient story continues to have implications for relationships in our own times, because it stresses the importance of kindness between partners. Couples who strive to treat each other kindly will have relationships that are mutually satisfying and fulfilling.

Create top-quality time together.

In today's hectic, busy world, many couples feel overwhelmed by daily duties. Without even being aware of it, they can end up living parallel and unconnected lives. Robert Stephan Cohen, a leading New York City divorce lawyer observes, "A couple might live in the same house and share the same bed, but their communication may be perfunctory. They could go for days without really talking. Whether because of busy career, childrearing, or even time-consuming hobbies, they never make time for each other." The strategy he recommends for couples so that they avoid the pitfall of parallel lives is to "carve out time for each other by picking one night a week to go on a date. That means time together—no phone calls or kids. Also, don't let a day go by without having a conversation, even if it is by phone." Cohen recalls one professional couple who had little free time for each other, so they decided to share part of every day by walking their dog together. That simple change put their marriage back on track.

Keep in mind that a date night doesn't need to be an expensive outing. The goal is to spend time together, not necessarily to spend a lot of money. Inexpensive activities for a date night could include any of the following:

- Taking out food from a favorite restaurant and enjoying it in a park.
- Taking an evening walk to enjoy the sunset together.
- Spending the evening at a roller rink or ice skating rink.
- Watching a favorite movie together.
- Walking through a mall to window shop then stopping for coffee.
- Miniature golfing or bowling (both are inexpensive, fun activities).
- Taking up a new hobby or sport together.
- Sending the kids to visit grandparents, other relatives, or friends so you and your spouse can have the evening alone at home.

- Hiring a babysitter from time to time for the sole purpose of freeing up an evening to be enjoyed as you and your partner desire.
- If you're both working, consider a lunchtime date.
- Visiting a local museum.
- Playing tourist in your own city and doing some sightseeing.

Be sure to explain to your children that it's important for parents to have time alone together and that it doesn't mean they are less important. Help them understand that family strength emerges when parents have a strong, stable relationship.

Creating top-quality time together is a basic ingredient of friendship. Deep and abiding friendships thrive and grow when people spend time together. Top-quality time will assure that you will remain each other's best friend. Jeanette C. Lauer and Robert H. Lauer, authors of *Til Death Do Us Part*, studied 351 couples who were married 15 years or more to determine what makes a marriage not only enduring but satisfying and happy. Of those responding, 300 of the couples indicated they were very happy in their marriages. They were asked to select from 39 factors and list in order of importance what they thought it was that made their marriage lasting and enjoyable. Approximately 90 percent of both husbands and wives put the same factor at the top of their list: *My spouse is my best friend*.

Eliminate bickering, blaming, and boredom.

As couples grow apart, they also tend to fall into an unhealthy pattern made up of three "B" words: *bickering, blaming, and boredom*. These are intimacy-killers. With a little intentional effort and consistency, this pattern can be broken and transformed. When you find yourself bickering, just stop. Discipline yourself to listen more and speak less. When you do talk, speak positively rather than negatively. When you catch yourself in a blaming mode, again, just stop. Remind yourself that blame is counterproductive. Finger-pointing and fault-finding do not open the door to a better relationship. Instead of blaming, find ways to improve yourself and how you're relating to your partner. Whenever you feel that your relationship is in a rut and boring, then use that as your wake-up call to take steps that will add vitality and energy to the relationship.

Consider the creative and spontaneous way one couple spices up their relationship. When it comes time to plan their vacation, they go to their local library where there is a world globe, three feet in diameter. One of them gives it a spin while the other closes his or her eyes and points. Wherever the finger lands, that's where they go on vacation. There are some rules that guide this process. Ocean locations can be either cruises or sailing vacations. Only one ocean vacation is permitted every four years. If an already visited location is chosen, the spinner gets to choose any adjacent country. War zones are omitted. Needless to say, this couple is adding great vitality to their marriage and, in the process, collecting wonderful experiences and shared memories.

Practice awareness, admiration, and acknowledgment.

Practicing awareness, admiration, and acknowledgment is advice that comes from psychiatrist Mark Goulston. In his book *The 6 Secrets of a Lasting Relationship*, he says couples must increase their level of appreciation for each other by practicing the following:

- *Awareness:* "If you look for things that are unacceptable, you can always find them; if you look for things to feel thankful for, you can always find those too. It's a matter of choosing what you want to look for."
- *Admiration:* "Your partner may have worked hard to develop some of the traits you like. It may take a good deal

of effort and commitment to live up to certain values or standards of behavior. It might require a good deal of compromise and sacrifice to make you happy or safeguard your family or preserve the dignity of your relationship. Those efforts are worthy of admiration."

- *Acknowledgment:* "Don't keep your appreciation to yourself. Express it to your partner."

To heighten your appreciation of your partner, Dr. Goulston reminds couples to become more intentional about this by carefully scrutinizing the good qualities their mate brings to the relationship. He notes that many times couples really don't understand the pressures a partner faces or the demands on his or her time and energy. To better understand and appreciate your mate, Dr. Goulston recommends asking yourself questions such as the following:

- Does he or she make sacrifices to improve our life together?
- Does he or she refrain from saying or doing certain things to keep the peace in our relationship?
- Does he or she work hard to be a better person?
- What compromises does he or she make on behalf of our relationship?
- What does he or she have to put up with to be with me?

Show that you truly love and cherish your partner.

On November 15, 1942, Louise Shimoff eagerly said "I do" to Marcus, her dashing groom who was proudly wearing a crisp, formal United States Army uniform. Only a short eight months later, he was called to serve in World War II, bound for an unknown destination in the Pacific for an unknown period of time. Louise and her husband would not see each other again for two years and four months. During that entire time, they were able to speak by telephone on only one occasion.

Yet when they were reunited, the couple was delighted to discover their love and commitment for each other was as strong and vibrant as ever. The glue that continued to bond their relationship despite the separation was one short sentence made up of three important words: *I love you*. Throughout the long days and nights of those war years, Louise and her husband wrote each other a total of 1,716 letters. Some days there was not much to write about, but in every single letter those three words, *I love you*, were included. Those letters and that important message carried both of them through the war. Since then, Louise and Marcus have celebrated more than 50 happy years together. Throughout their long marriage, Louise and Marcus have continued to show each other the same love and devotion that characterized the early years of their marriage.

Clearly, Louise and Marcus know how to practice the fine art of staying in love. Their ability to do so has resulted in a satisfying and fulfilling marriage. Like all happily married couples, they know a relationship is a living, growing organism. Neglected, it will wither up and die. Nurtured, it will constantly replenish and renew.

Avoid at all costs the issue faced by some people of taking their partner and their marriage for granted. If this begins in your relationship, then begin immediately to extend the same courtesies and expressions of love that were present at the start of the relationship. Author and physician Adeline Yen Mah has been married for three decades to her husband, Bob. "Right from the beginning, and throughout our time together, he has been caring and true. In the whole of my life I have never encountered anyone so loving or felt so cherished," she explains. As an anesthesiologist, she is often called to the hospital for emergency operations that are stressful and frequently last all night. "No matter what time I came home, however, I would find the dinner cooked and my husband waiting for me. Sometimes, he'd be so exhausted he would doze off while we ate."

Dr. Yen Mah receives many invitations to speak and without hesitation, Bob always accompanies her. "Because of him, these occasions became minivacations rather than stressful obligations," she adds. "The knowledge of his presence is indescribably comforting and means everything in the world to me. Every day he shows me tokens of his love."

Shower your partner with praise and compliments.

Love thrives and deepens when praise is present. Just imagine how pleased Cindy Hensley McCain, wife of United States Senator John McCain, felt when she read his glowing words about her in his book *Worth Fighting For:*

> Cindy and I were married the following May (1980) and I have wondered over my good fortune ever since. She has compounded my blessings many times over, with the birth of our first daughter, Meghan, our two sons, Jack and Jimmy, and the adoption of our daughter Bridget. She has enriched my life beyond measure, making my successes and my defeats of much less consequence than my happiness at home.

Whenever you spot something admirable or noble or lovely in your partner, comment on it. And remember to offer praise in front of others. Compliments received when others hear them are doubly pleasing. Praise is verbal sunshine and causes relationships to blossom and grow.

Another person who knows how to affirm and praise his partner is former United States President Jimmy Carter. Of course, he automatically receives a great deal of attention. Yet he is quick to acknowledge and praise the contributions of his wife, Rosalynn. Their leadership through the Carter Center in Atlanta is "almost entirely among the poorest and most needy people, in this country and in foreign nations. . . . Rosalynn is a full partner with me, and she has been in charge of our efforts in the field of mental health. Under her leadership, more than sixty formerly uncooperative organizations now come together annually to share their common ideas and goals." Clearly, Jimmy Carter views his wife as an equal, and they are teammates in their projects.

Balance your roles as partners and parents.

In her book *Woman First: Family Always*, Kathryn Sansone writes,

> It's easy for parents today to get swept up in their children's lives. From the minute we take them home, put on their first diapers, and give them their first bottles, we begin trying our best to fulfill all of our children's needs and demands. While I am a firm believer in being a thoughtful, committed parent, I also know that if couples don't put their relationship first (most of the time), then no amount of devotion to their kids will keep their relationship alive.

As the mother of 10 children, Sansone knows "it's not easy to keep a healthy balance between thinking of ourselves as both partners and parents." Yet she stresses the importance of husband and wives doing just that:

> The best gift you can give your children is a loving relationship with your spouse. When children know—and witness—their parents putting aside time for each other, kids understand that their parents are committed to each other. They also know that their parents love each other. In turn, this love between their parents makes kids feel safe, enabling them to grow unhindered, following their own unique destinies.

Schedule physical intimacy.

Putting sex on your calendar may seem to lack spontaneity, but it is a technique that works for many couples. One woman who was seeing a counselor poured out her marital frustrations.

She wanted more sexual intimacy from her husband, but he was overwhelmed with work and parenting responsibilities. "As the parents of four active children, we can hardly find time for ourselves outside the bedroom, let alone inside the bedroom. Basically, we've become roommates, not lovers." When the counselor suggested they schedule intimacy on their calendars, the woman laughed, saying, "Sex is supposed to be spontaneous, not scheduled!" Nevertheless, the woman told her husband about the counselor's suggestion. They acted on her advice and are now successfully restoring intimacy in their marriage.

Even if you feel like the woman did, that sex should be spontaneous and not scheduled, consider these nine benefits of scheduling intimacy:

1. It eliminates begging. If one partner has a higher sexual desire, that partner is often requesting physical intimacy more often. It can leave that person feeling as though he or she is too needy or begging for intimacy.

2. It removes the fear of rejection. When intimacy is scheduled for a specific day or evening, the fear of rejection is eliminated. A common reason many couples cease enjoying physical intimacy is fear of rejection.

3. It eliminates guessing. Does she want to? Is he up for it? A schedule completely removes the guesswork. It's a done deal.

4. It builds desire. According to psychologists, the strongest sex organ is the brain. When a date for sexual intimacy is scheduled, the brain becomes engaged and prepares the rest of the body for the activity. Once on the calendar, it becomes a reminder to start thinking about sex, priming partners to "get in the mood."

5. It taps into prime time. She likes to have sex right before bedtime, but he is usually too tired then. This couple can decide that once a week they will schedule their physical intimacy for Fridays at 8 P.M., a time frame that works well for both partners.

6. It increases anticipation. Scheduling physical intimacy keeps it forefront in the relationship. Both partners eagerly look forward to that time together.

7. It reminds couples to prepare physically. A hot bath or shower, shaving, creams, and perfumes are comfortable, relaxing ways to prepare for sexual intimacy.

8. It builds trust. When husband and wife make the commitment, it is one that must be kept. Both spouses must honor the agreement, be present, and be available.

9. It prioritizes the importance of intimacy. Nothing else detracts from the scheduled intimacy date. Other invitations are declined, and the phone is left unanswered.

Always be flexible and patient.

A relationship is a living, vital, and changing organism. Be prepared to go with the flow and the changes that emerge over time. "Marriages aren't made in heaven. They're made over a period of years of sacrifice, thoughtfulness, and work," notes Fred Matheny, a writer and husband for three decades. "The chief thing is that people change. They develop different agendas. They want to do different things, and you have to accommodate these differences within the relationship—where you live, how much money you spend, all these things. They have to be worked out. You have to communicate." Flexibility and patience result in marital rewards that are mutually beneficial.

One woman shares the success that came as a result of her patience and flexibility. Her husband was not emotionally expressive. "He was not a touchy, feely, huggy kind of man, but this was something I deeply wanted," she says. The woman exercised flexibility by reining in her high expectations while at the same time showering him with verbal "I love you's" as well as touching, hugging, and kissing him even if he turned away. She also practiced patience by continuing to give him what she hoped he could give back.

It has paid off for both of them. She says, "My husband has become much more emotionally expressive and physically demonstrative. This was not easy for him, as he had a difficult childhood. He was abandoned when he was eight years old and placed in 14 different foster homes over the years. I knew it was difficult for him to trust people and to physically or verbally show his love. Yet I believed in 'us' and remained patient and consistent in showing him and telling him that he was important and valuable to me. He has learned to show and verbalize his love for me as well as our children through hugs, kisses and verbal expressions."

Tap into your faith to deepen your marriage.

A woman tells of a simple spiritual experiment she conducted. Like many families, life had become hectic, and she found herself busy with work, parenting, and volunteering. What slipped away in their marriage was a focus on the spiritual. She decided to spend a few minutes every day for one month praying specifically for her husband. There wasn't a specific problem she was praying about; she just wanted to be supportive of her husband in his activities. She prayed for his commute to work, for his encounters with colleagues and clients, that God would bless him throughout the day. She didn't tell her husband about her experiment, but interestingly, he began to confide more and more in her, asking her to pray about situations he had never mentioned before. She discovered that her simple experiment in prayer brought them even closer together.

Family faith is a vital ingredient for marital happiness and closeness. It's also an invaluable resource when problems emerge. The great success of Alcoholics Anonymous and other 12-step programs come from acknowledging there is a higher power and calling upon that power for aid. The same principle applies to marital issues: couples who draw upon and turn to God will increase their ability to meet challenges, solve problems, and move from feeling helpless to being helped. If you're facing issues in your relationship or if it seems to be floundering, try applying these biblical passages to break a marital impasse:

- *To cultivate greater compassion,* apply Eph. 4:32: "Be kind and compassionate to one another, forgiving each other, just as in Christ God forgave you."

- *To help love flow more freely,* review and act upon 1 Cor. 13:4-8: "Love is patient, love is kind. It does not envy, it does not boast, it is not proud. It is not rude, it is not self-seeking, it is not easily angered, it keeps no record of wrongs. Love does not delight in evil but rejoices with the truth. It always protects, always trusts, always hopes, always perseveres. Love never fails."

- *When one of you is definitely in the wrong,* follow the advice of James 5:16: "Confess your sins to each other and pray for each other so that you [or your relationship] may be healed."

- *When forgiveness is called for, but you feel unwilling,* remember that Jesus said to Peter when Peter asked how many times we're supposed to forgive, "I tell you, not seven times, but seventy-seven times" (Matt. 18:22). Keep in mind that Jesus is really saying that we must cultivate a capacity to forgive that's unlimited and unreserved.

- *When angry,* hold back and apply the advice of James 1:19—"Everyone should be quick to listen, slow to speak and slow to become angry."

- *If resentment emerges,* consider Paul's advice to husbands (and it applies equally to wives) in Col. 3:19—"Husbands, love your wives and do not be harsh with them." Wives, don't forget that this verse applies to you as well and could just as easily say for you to love your husbands and not to be harsh with them.

- *When tempted to lash out at your partner,* soften your emotions by remembering the words of King Solomon: "A gentle answer turns away wrath, but a harsh word stirs up anger. The tongue of the wise commends knowledge, but the mouth of the fool gushes folly" (Prov. 15:1-2).

Of course, couples can head off many problems and issues when their faith life is vital and shared. Some ways of doing that include studying the Bible together, attending worship as a couple or family, praying for each other and praying together, offering forgiveness and acceptance, and supporting each other to grow, change, and expand. Mutual faith and common spiritual goals will provide a strong, stable foundation for your relationship, allowing it to weather various issues and differences that can emerge from time to time.

Finally, if the marriage is struggling and the going gets tough, never give in to despair. Rather, turn to God, seeking His guidance and help. Remember that your pastor or a Christian counselor can help you regain the intimacy you once cherished. And listen to the Word of God spoken through the prophet Jeremiah in Jer. 31:3-4: "I have loved you with an everlasting love; I have drawn you with loving-kindness. *I will build you up again and you will be rebuilt*" (emphasis added). With God all things are possible. Damaged marriages can be healed.

Victor M. Parachin, an ordained minister, has served as a pastor in Washington, D.C., and Chicago and has provided interim ministry in Los Angeles and Tulsa, Oklahoma. Currently he is a full-time freelance writer. He has authored 10 books and written numerous articles appearing in national and regional newspapers and magazines.

Books include *Ties That Bind: Remaining Happy as a Couple After the Wedding* (Chalice Press), *Healing Grief* (Chalice Press), *Grief Relief* (Chalice Press), *Daily Strength: One Year of Inspiration from the Bible* (Liguori Triumph Books)

7 Finding Spiritual Intimacy in Your Marriage

JIM PETTITT AND JEANETTE DOWNS PETTITT

"WE SHARE EVERYTHING—WE SHARE NOTHING!" It is a confusing statement on the surface, but full of truth when it comes to spiritual intimacy in marriage. Couples who enjoy the same recreation, watch the same television shows, share daily information about their jobs, raise their children together, and laugh and cry together often have difficulty sharing their spiritual needs and desires with each other.

The above quote is from a couple married 24 years with three children who attend church, claim a vital relationship with Jesus Christ, and serve faithfully in church leadership positions. They pray together from time to time, have their own private devotions, and thoroughly enjoy worshiping together in Sunday services. They hesitantly admit, however, that they rarely talk with each other about their own personal, inner spiritual thoughts and journeys. He says simply, "I see the results of her spirituality, but she has seldom let me in where that spirituality lives. I feel as if there's a whole piece of her that's walled off from me that I can never share."

In the counseling experiences in my office, I have found this more the rule than the exception. Our spiritual journeys are the most private areas of existence and are expressions of the core of our beings as creations of God. Precisely because of its importance to who we are as persons, discussions of our spirituality requires a high level of vulnerability and the possibility of deep hurt. In too many cases we shy away from the deep discussions that could bring us together and settle for surface relationships in this vitally important area of our married lives.

In Eph. 5 Paul suggests that the marriage relationship can be the earthly reflection of Christ's relationship with us. In discussing the wife's relationship with her husband, Paul uses the words "as Christ is the head of the Church" (v. 23), and in regard to the husband's relationship to his wife he again says "just as Christ loved the church" (v. 25). When that level of intimacy exists in a marriage relationship, there's no holding back any area of life. All areas are to be known by both parties and to be under the leadership of Christ. Verse 31 underscores this level of intimacy by referencing and echoing the "one flesh" relationship mentioned in Gen. 2:24.

For our marriages to reflect the intimacy that exists between Christ and the Church, we must share with our spouses the innermost part of who we are and what we hope to become. The question then becomes "How can my marriage reach that point?"

In our quest for true spiritual intimacy in our marriages, we'll first look at the essential, foundational stones upon which spiritual intimacy is built. Then we will proceed to look at some of the traits and exercises that will help create and maintain spiritual intimacy in a marriage relationship.

HE IS MY LORD

Spiritual intimacy in a Christian marriage begins with each partner having made a commitment to Christ. This commitment to Christ calls each of us to recognize His personal leadership or lordship over our lives. What does it mean to have Christ as Lord? When Christ is Lord, then all we have, all we are belongs to Him. He is our master, our leader, our Savior.

In his letter to the Roman church, Paul describes what he sees as our proper response to the sacrifice of Christ: "I urge you, brothers, in view of God's mercy, to offer your bodies as living sacrifices, holy and pleasing to God—this is your spiritual act of worship" (Rom. 12:1). Paul's statement about the place God should have in our lives leaves little room for negotiation. We're to consider ourselves His from our wallet to our wrinkles. However, that's not the full story. Christ did not come as Lord to abuse us. No, His love for us is His motivation. Jesus reveals his intentions in John 10:10 when He declares, "I have come that they may have life, and have it to the full."

So when we give ourselves to Christ, we begin a lifelong journey of receiving the blessings of God. That journey will have its challenges and its joys; its hardships and victories. However, as God's child, we will never walk alone. Everywhere we travel we are in the presence of the Holy Spirit. The Holy Spirit's presence enables us to become who we need to become in order to fulfill God's calling on our lives, even to the relationship we have with our spouses.

In the third chapter of Colossians Paul says that, as "God's chosen people, holy and dearly loved" (v. 12), we can become persons who—

- Are clothed with gentleness, kindness, humility, and compassion (v. 12).
- Have the grace to put up with all the unique idiosyncrasies of those we love and offer forgiveness when needed (v. 13).
- Have hearts that are ruled by peace, the very peace of the Lord himself (v. 15).
- Are guided by the Word of God, which dwells in our hearts in all its richness (v. 16).
- Seeks His will in everything we do, especially in marriage (v. 17).

Paul's prayer for the early Christians reveals how much difference having Christ as Lord can make in one's life. He prays for Christians in 1 Thess. 3:12—"May the Lord make your love increase and overflow for each other." He also prays in Col.

3:14, "Over all these virtues put on love, which binds them all together in perfect unity." That unity is what couples seek in marriage. That unity is possible when we yield ourselves fully to Christ our Lord.

HE IS OUR LORD

One of the first issues a couple recognizes when they desire more spiritual intimacy in their marriage is that even though each one has made a personal commitment to Christ, that commitment does not automatically translate into marital spiritual harmony. They think that one Christian woman plus one Christian man equals one Christian marriage with all the perks and privileges. Unfortunately, that's not the case. For a couple to have a Christian marriage, they must bring their marriage under the Lordship of Christ. In most cases, that requires an intentional act of commitment to God and each other.

Such a commitment is well illustrated in Rom. 12:1. In this verse we read that we are to offer our lives as sacrifices to Christ. We are to be obedient to His call, be ready to suffer for His sake, to love others as He has loved us, and live as He calls us to live. Each of these actions requires a conscious decision of the will by both marriage partners. When it comes to making this offering to God within our marriage, we face several questions:

- How can I speak for the other person?
- What must be done for us to be obedient as a couple?
- How do we cooperate in such an intimate endeavor?
- Where do we begin?

These and other questions will be addressed as we proceed through the chapter. Let's start with an issue Paul considered crucial. Ephesians 5:21 highlights one of the key elements necessary for the development of spiritual intimacy: mutual submission. Paul writes, "Submit to one another out of reverence for Christ." The concept of submission in marriage has received a bad reputation—in some cases deservedly so. Too often Paul's comments on submission are taken out of context and portrayed as dominance of one person over the other. This common misconception ignores his original call to mutual submission (5:21) and becomes a one-sided discussion of male authority. This distorted definition misses the point of the Ephesians passage and makes a mockery of Lordship altogether.

The New Testament concept of submission is difficult for couples to grasp, because it flies in the face of contemporary insistence on privacy and individuality. Couples have become so engrossed in the pursuit of their own "rights" that it's difficult or impossible for them to think in terms of *us* in the relationship. Too many married individuals are interested in finding personal fulfillment, feeding individual needs, and maintaining self identity. They often see anything that forces them to give up personal rights and privileges as the enemy of their happiness. They monitor the value of their relationships by asking such questions as "What can the other person do to make me happy?" or "What am I getting out of this relationship?" The focus is on the individual and not the marriage partnership.

However, under the Lordship of Christ, each person is called to be other-focused. The apostle Paul does this in Eph. 5 by calling for mutual submission. Mutual submission means that both husband and wife must look at the relationship through the thoughts, values, needs, and desires of the other person. In speaking to the husband, Paul says that he should consider his wife's needs and desires as being the same as if they were his own. The wife is to submit in the same way to the needs of her husband, learning what he desires and needs and doing her best to fulfill them as allowed under the Lordship of Christ.

In this attitude of mutual submission, each spouse shows ultimate respect and love for the other. Each knows that he or she is valued, loved, and cared for by his or her spouse. Mutual submission also brings a couple into obedience to the Word of God, a crucial step toward bringing their marriage under the Lordship of Christ.

Mutual submission changes the way we relate to each other as children of God and shows the world that our relationship is truly different. When our relationship is brought into obedience to God, and the Holy Spirit fills us with all the fullness of God, we'll see significant changes in how we talk with each other, how we react toward each other, how we seek to understand each other, and how we live in an attitude of forgiveness toward each other. None of these can be done consistently without a holy submission to God and each other.

VITAL AREAS OF MUTUAL SUBMISSION

Conversation

When we submit to the Lordship of Christ, we must also bring conversation under His guidance. According to Paul, God would have us speak to each other in loving truthfulness. In Eph. 4:15 we are told to "[speak] the truth in love." Under the Lordship of Christ, couples would never intentionally and deliberately hurt the other with words.

Hurting his wife was clearly the motive of the young man who sat across from Jeanette and me in an evening counseling session. Both husband and wife were hurting from years of arguments and marital difficulties. Tearfully, the young woman shared some of the pain she had suffered in the relationship, some of which he was not even aware. As she spoke, we could see the red rising in his face until he looked as if he might explode, which he did. For the next several minutes he filled the room with accusations, vilifications, insults, with some curse words thrown in for good measure. At the end of his tirade, he topped it off with the statement "I'm just telling the truth."

In fact, he *was* telling the truth. Over the preceding several sessions it had become evident that she was responsible for the many hurts he expressed. But there was no love in his telling the truth. The young man was using truth as a weapon to hurt, to control, and to force her to see how bad she was. It was truth swathed in hatred and ugliness and could in no way be seen as an imitation of God and His redeeming love for us. He was acting emotionally, striking back at his wife because of the emotional pain he had experienced.

The good news is that some months later he confessed to me that he had recognized the ugliness and evil of his truth-telling incident. While he had told the truth, he knew he had told the truth to get even with his wife. He shared with me that by reflecting on his emotional response he had learned that he needed to commit his conversational habits to God. He then went to his wife and asked for forgiveness. In a later counseling session he expressed the same hurts to his wife in a redemptive and loving manner, and God brought true healing to their relationship. When I see them now, it's hard to believe they're the same couple.

In Eph. 4:29 we're told, "Do not let any unwholesome talk come out of your mouths, but only what is helpful for building others up according to their needs, that it may benefit those who listen." Here Paul tells us that our conversation as Christians under the Lordship of Christ should build up the other person.

Even criticism can be done in a way that encourages the other person. Jeanette, my wife, approached me not too long ago with these words: "We need to talk." She began talking about my teaching in the Sunday School class with several words of praise from other class members, and she told me how much she liked my teaching and what she liked about it the most. Then, almost as an aside, she suggested that I was being more "preachy" than usual and that it tended to take away from my real gift of involving class members in the lesson. By the time she got to the criticism, I felt like the greatest teacher in the world (though I know I'm not). And I went away from the critique with the same message. What a loving way to say "You're talking too much"!

The second principle Paul mentions is that when we're critiquing another person, his or her needs—not ours—should be at the center of the conversation. All too often the purpose of our criticism is to get the other person to act the way we want him or her to act or think the way we want him or her to think. However, our first concern should be to encourage the person by communicating our acceptance and love of who he or she is, even when improvement is needed. When criticism demonstrates this attitude of love and acceptance, then the recipient of the critique is much more likely to accept the word of correction and challenge.

In Rom. 14:19 Paul, talking about how mature Christians should speak to each other, suggests that in our conversation we should "make every effort" to bring peace and build each other up. In Matt. 12:36-37 Jesus warns that we will be judged for every careless word we speak and that those words represent our true inner character. Under the Lordship of Christ, our aim must always be for our conversations with our spouses to be loving and kind.

Dealing with Our Emotions

In relating with each other as husband and wife, we run the full range of human emotions. These emotions include joy, happiness, delight, elation, and many others. They also include the more painful or darker emotions such as anger, frustration, hurt, disappointment, and fear. Since it is the darker emotions that give us the most challenge in the marriage relationship, we'll focus our attention there.

More often than not, the emotion that gives us the most difficulty in our relationships and conversations is anger. Anger can be communicated and interpreted in multiple ways. We can be angry because we're hurt, frustrated, or disappointed. When our spouses experience our anger, their initial response is often defensiveness. As a result, the issue that should have been the topic of discussion is lost in the emotional fog of the moment. The energy that should have been used to resolve the issue is used up dissipating the anger.

When we make comments that tear another person down, it's very destructive. We think we'll feel better if we win the verbal conflict, but the victory is short-lived and comes at a very high price.

When anger is allowed to fester, it can lead to what I call the "anger sins" that Paul catalogs in Eph. 4:31. While the immediate emotion or anger goes away, the hurt does not. Hurt builds upon hurt, frustration upon frustration, disappointment upon disappointment, building a mountain of resentment. When this occurs, we no longer respond with simple anger but with explosions of unreasonable anger that are both audible and inaudible. If the anger builds long enough, it can become resentment and bitterness. The sad thing about bitterness is that it comes from a heart that's no longer hot with anger but a heart that's turned cold and calculating. Love has no harbor in such a polluted environment.

Paul says there's no place for unresolved anger in a relationship under the Lordship of Christ. In Eph. 4:26 Paul says that while we can be angry (it is a God-given emotion), the anger should not lead us into sin. In verse 31 he admonishes us to purge ourselves of those things that come from anger, such as bitterness, rage, brawling, and saying hurtful things about the other person. Purging ourselves of anger is not often done just by a single miraculous transformation. More often than not, freedom from the negative effects of anger comes as a result of a continuing partnership of our will and the Holy Spirit.

If you've accumulated years of unresolved anger and developed the habit of responding to others in anger, you may need to seek the help of a pastor or counselor to help you establish new habits and skills that will enable you to respond to your spouse in love.

Controlling one's emotions is a sign of emotional and spiritual maturity, and maturing requires both time and effort. This maturing process may take work, but the benefit will be well worth the effort, because it's one of the essential pathways to spiritual intimacy with your spouse.

COMPASSION AND FORGIVENESS

Another key element of intimate relationships is addressed by Paul in Eph. 4:32 when he states, "Be kind and compassionate to one another, forgiving each other, just as in Christ God forgave you." It's through God's kindness, compassion, and forgiveness that we began our relationship with Him. Scripture reveals that God loved us so much that He invested himself in our situations, giving up His Son as the sin offering for us. Now that's compassion! When we began to personally experience God's compassion and forgiveness, our relationship with Him became intimate.

That's also true in the marriage relationship. Spiritual intimacy is grounded in the investment spouses make in one another. When we invest in meeting the needs of our spouses, our marriage relationships blossom on every level.

How many times do we invest in our relationships with our spouses by meeting them at their point of need? When we come home from work, do we see how we can help lift their loads by helping out, or do we quickly escape to our favorite hobby or to the TV room? Compassion calls us to personal involvement—to notice the need and become involved.

Compassion also requires that we listen to and understand our spouses. If we desire to have an intimate marriage, we'll need to shift our attention to our spouses. Too often we're so wrapped up in our own needs that we rarely have time to consider the needs of our spouses. Sometimes our neglect is the result of selfishness, or we simply don't take the time to listen. We must put our empathy into action. Empathy in action is the fruit of compassion.

While exercising compassion is crucially important to developing a spiritually intimate marriage, practicing forgiveness is essential as well. Marriage is certain to be punctuated with failures, misunderstandings, times when we miss the mark. In those times we must practice forgiveness, seek forgiveness when we need it, and extend forgiveness when we have been wronged.

Forgiveness is a full partner to love and compassion and is commanded by Scripture in Eph. 4:32. Jesus taught that God's forgiveness is contingent upon our forgiveness of others. "When you stand praying, if you hold anything against anyone, forgive him, so that your Father in heaven may forgive you your sins" (Mark 11:25). That should provide motivation to us who are slow to forgive others.

Forgiveness becomes increasingly difficult if we've spent years hanging on to every wrong our spouses have committed and allowed them to accumulate in our hearts and minds. One couple I worked with was extremely difficult to counsel, because they had been hurting each other for more than 10 years. Whenever a subject was presented for discussion in our counseling sessions, one of them would angrily remember a hurt or disappointment he or she had experienced from the other. Every discussion seemed to explode into an argument. I learned through those sessions that resolving issues quickly and moving on is an essential of marital health. It's nearly impossible to restore marital health if the partners are holding on to 10, 20, or even 30 years of unresolved and unforgiven wrongdoing.

When we're fully yielded to the Lordship of Christ, we give up the right to be right and learn to extend forgiveness freely.

For many couples, learning to forgive is the first step to making progress on establishing spiritual intimacy. There can be no true spiritual intimacy where there's no forgiveness,

Forgiveness within marriage often follows a predictable path. First, the offense must be recognized. Naming it helps bring clarity to the process and paves a path to reconciliation. This simple process of recognizing the issue and communicating it enables both parties to accept responsibility for their actions and to strategize how to prevent further harm.

Next, we bring our attitudes and actions into harmony with our statements of forgiveness. It's common for us to occasionally feel a resurgence of anger toward the party we've forgiven. However, forgiveness, like love, is an act of will, and our feelings of forgiveness and acceptance will follow in time. It's also wise to remember that acts of forgiveness are acts of obedience and submission to Christ. Forgiving our spouses will bring a sense of spiritual victory to our hearts and minds, because through our actions we're fulfilling God's plan for marriage.

Finally, if we seek a truly intimate relationship with our husbands or wives, we must give up our right to justice. Isaiah 66:16 says, "The LORD will execute judgment." That is not our right. Scripture precludes our requiring justice in our relationships. We are, in our marriages, to mirror Christ and His relationship to the Church. That means that in place of justice we choose to extend mercy and grace to the other person. And that extension of mercy and grace flows best from a forgiven and forgiving heart.

Bringing ourselves and our marriages under the Lordship of Christ sets the stage for a growing sense of spiritual intimacy. Modeling our relationships after Christ's relationship with the Church allows our relationships to mature in an atmosphere of respect, kindness, compassion, admiration, compassion, and forgiveness. In this atmosphere we can begin to share our spiritual journeys hand in hand with our spouses.

MARRIAGE AND SPIRITUAL INTIMACY

It would seem that when our relationships are committed to Christ and we're living in obedience to His Word, spiritual intimacy would naturally follow. However, in a broken and sinful world, the sharing of our innermost spiritual thoughts isn't always easy. Even when we consciously bring our marriages to Christ and ask Him to be the head of our relationships, we can find that building spiritual intimacy within our marriages is challenging. With this in mind, let's look at what we can do to develop spiritual intimacy with our spouses.

Unconditional Acceptance

Dennis Rainey, in his book *Building Your Mate's Self-Esteem*, says the greatest fear we have in our relationships is the fear of rejection. With that in mind, it's understandable why couples fear sharing their spiritual lives with each other.

Lisa grew up in a family where no feeling was sacred and exempt from criticism. Early in their marriage John would try to engage her in conversations regarding her relationship with God. As a young man he had dreamed of deep, engaging times of sharing the love and blessings of God with his wife. Lisa would listen to him, but when he tried to get her to talk, she withdrew and grew quiet and refused to answer his questions. It finally came to the point that he even questioned whether she was a Christian and began to think he had made a mistake in marrying her. Out of desperation, they sought counseling from a Christian therapist.

In one session Lisa was able to share what she had experienced in her family. As John listened, he began to understand that she was afraid he would not accept her spirituality as good enough, and she feared he might even make fun of her for how she saw God and worshiped Him. In the safety of the therapist's presence, she began to share small portions of her walk with Christ with John and experienced his acceptance with a sense of awe and wonder.

Since only God can read the heart and know who loves Him and who does not, we need to accept and validate the spiritual journeys of our spouses. It's dangerous to assume that because someone's spiritual journey is different than ours it's somehow less than ours. God has made each of us unique, and that uniqueness often causes us to react to life and relate to God differently.

In Gary L. Thomas's book *Sacred Pathways*, he suggests there are many different ways that individuals relate to God. Our personalities, cultures, backgrounds, and temperaments shape the way we relate to Him. Thomas suggests, for example, that one person might feel closest to God as they participate in the great rituals and traditions of the Church. The rituals and traditions give them a sense of God's power and holiness. On the other hand, one might feel closest to God when he or she is meeting the spiritual and physical needs of others through service. Other pathways are worship, contemplation, nature, worship, study, and fellowship.

Rob and Terri were very different from John and Lisa. Both were willing to share with each other about how they viewed God and their walk with Christ. Rob never felt closer to God than when he was with other Christians. He marveled at the presence of God in the church services, talked about religious things with his friends, and came home from church activities rejuvenated and excited about serving the Lord. He noticed that Terri seemed uncomfortable in large crowds and often withdrew to a corner of the room and picked up a good Christian book or the Bible and lost herself in it. He sensed she was reluctant to engage in the fellowship activities and preferred to stay home. Soon they began to resent each other. Rob felt Terri was holding him back spiritually because she did not like to attend all the opportunities for church fellowship. Terri, on the other hand, felt Rob was pushing her to become something she was not by asking her to go to the church events. He deemed her as less than spiritual because she didn't want to be with other Christians; she viewed his spirituality as shallow and dependent on others.

Finally, after an intense argument, they sought counseling from their pastor. After filling out a personality inventory, they discovered that Rob was extroverted by nature and Terri was an introvert. Their pastor helped Rob understand that Terri needed to worship God through personal reading of the Word and private contemplation. He helped Terri understand that Rob needed fellowship with other Christians to grow and stay spiritually engaged. Their sessions helped them value their differences and respect each other as unique individuals.

One preference of communicating and experiencing God's presence is not better than another. If our desire is to become soulmates, we need to allow our spouses to be who God designed them to be. Acceptance is crucial to developing spiritual intimacy. When we accept their spiritual journeys, we're helping them feel comfortable enough to share their inmost thoughts and feelings, and spiritual intimacy will follow.

Risking

No amount of acceptance can bring about spiritual intimacy unless we're willing to risk being vulnerable. At some point in time we must be willing to risk being hurt or rejected. This is especially true when we are sharing information about our spiritual lives with our spouses.

Jesus took significant risks sharing His life and thoughts with those significant to Him. Many times He opened himself to His disciples, only to be disappointed when they missed the point or rejected the truth He shared. Remember when He tried to share with the disciples His impending death? Peter rejected the plan because it did not fit his idea of what the Christ should be. How that must have hurt Jesus, to know that His closest companions, the disciples, still did not understand or accept

Him for who He really was! But He did not give up on them. He knew that love would win and that they would eventually realize the truth of His words. We need to have the same attitude toward sharing ourselves with our spouses.

We must take the risk to share with our loved ones. Becoming open and vulnerable gives them the opportunity to understand and accept us for who we really are. No matter how many hurts we may have experienced from others, no matter how many times we may have been rejected, if we're to have intimate, spiritual relationships with our spouses, we must be willing to risk sharing our spiritual lives with them. So if your sharing has been misunderstood or rejected, try again.

Spiritual Disciplines

John Wesley was a champion of Methodism, a disciplined path to spiritual growth. Paul would also tell us that we cannot forget the centrality and importance of the spiritual disciplines. Colossians 3:16 lists three important disciplines that lead to spiritual growth: The Word of Christ, worship, and prayer. These spiritual activities help Christian couples acknowledge Christ as Lord of their lives.

First, God's Word is to dwell in us. As we study the Word of God together, it begins to become a part of our relationship. And since we're spiritual partners, we can lead each other into spiritual growth. Years ago, Jeanette, my wife, shared with me the story of her first husband's death from diabetes. She told me that 1 Pet. 5:7 sustained her and her husband through the time of great pain and loss. As I looked at the verse through her hurt and suffering, I came to a new appreciation of Peter's words "Cast all your anxiety on him because he cares for you." Through her sharing that with me, our hearts became closer than ever before. Married couples often find this to be true when they share scripture together.

Second, it's important that couples worship together. During the worship service couples can communicate with each other as God speaks through the various elements of the service. In a counseling session, Tom shared that often in the service his wife, Rita, would reach over and squeeze his arm or hand or scoot closer and smile at him. When he asked her why she did that, she shared that the song or a point in the message had really moved her and that she wanted to share that moment with him. He soon realized that by "listening" for those times when she felt particularly moved, he was learning what made Rita "tick" spiritually. He also began to communicate in a similar manner with her, and their worship began to bring them both into a new awareness of each other's spiritual life.

Third, we should pray together as a couple. It is often said that prayer is conversation with God. When we pray together as a couple, that prayer becomes a three-way conversation. We're communicating not only with God but also with each other.

Matt said it took time for him to become comfortable praying in front of his wife. After many weeks of praying together, one day she told him, "I really appreciate your relationship with God. Because we're so different and respond differently spiritually, I sometimes wondered how close to God you really were. But as we prayed together, I began to realize that you have a wonderful and unique relationship to Christ. It has helped me to appreciate our own relationship even more."

If a couple wants to accelerate their spiritual growth, they should practice praying together. There's no better way to learn each other's hearts than to share in prayer. And remember that Jesus promised, "Where two or three come together in my name, there am I with them" (Matt. 18:20).

While it's not advisable to create a cookie-cutter mold for spiritual growth, some central disciplines should be observed by every couple. Observing these spiritual disciplines will help every couple mature spiritually as husband and wife and bring many opportunities for spiritual communication.

CONCLUSION

We've learned that lordship and spiritual intimacy in marriage are inseparable and intermingled. You can't have one without the other. Bringing life and the marriage relationship under the Lordship of Christ helps create an atmosphere of safety and trust—an essential of spiritual intimacy. When our self-revelations are treated with kindness and consideration, trust grows, and the depth of our sharing blossoms. The longer we look at our spouses through eyes of compassion, we'll be better able to extend forgiveness for the inevitable hurts that are a part of marriage relationships. We'll also have faith that the other person will forgive us, just as we forgive him or her. Even when we're angry or disagree, we can respond in love and acceptance. Every time we leave the presence of our spouses feeling special and loved, we find it easier to let them see us as we really are.

Sharon expressed it eloquently to me in a counseling session. "When I'm really feeling down and things are not going well, I immediately want to find my husband and tell him about it. I know that when our conversation is finished, my spirit will be lifted, I'll feel loved, and my world will be right-side-up again. I feel I could tell him anything about me and it would be accepted and valued."

Once we have committed our marriages to Christ and committed ourselves to being Christlike in our relationships, we can accept the spirituality of the other person and risk the vulnerability that will let our spouses see our souls. Perhaps this is what's really at the heart of becoming what so many married couples seek—"soul mates."

Jim Pettitt is currently the coordinator of Family Life Ministries for the Church of the Nazarene and adjunct professor of psychology at Johnson County (Kansas) Community College. Before taking his present responsibility, Jim taught courses for pastoral care and counseling at Nazarene Theological Seminary, was director of the Christian Counseling Center of Wichita, Kansas, and pastored Nazarene churches in Texas and Kansas. He speaks at men's retreats and family seminars.

Jeanette Downs Pettitt is director of the Career Center at MidAmerica Nazarene University and teaches in the MNU adult degree completion program. Jeanette has taught English at the high school level and at Olivet Nazarene University and has been a professional counselor for many years. She speaks at women's retreats, business seminars, and inspirational gatherings.

Jim and Jeanette travel across the country leading district and local marriage enrichment seminars and retreats.